MW00785886

MOBILE-MINDFUL TEACHING AND LEARNING

MOBILE-MINDFUL
TEACHING AND LEARNING

Harnessing the Technology That Students Use Most

Christina Moore

Foreword by Jenae Cohn

STERLING, VIRGINIA

COPYRIGHT © 2023 BY STYLUS PUBLISHING, LLC.

Published by Stylus Publishing, LLC.
22883 Quicksilver Drive
Sterling, Virginia 20166-2019

All rights reserved. No part of this book may be reprinted or reproduced in any form or by any electronic, mechanical, or other means, now known or hereafter invented, including photocopying, recording, and information storage and retrieval, without permission in writing from the publisher.

Library of Congress Cataloging-in-Publication-Data

Names: Moore, Christina (Ph.D.), author. | Cohn, Jenae, writer of foreword.
Title: Mobile-mindful teaching and learning : harnessing the technology that students use
    most / Christina Moore ; foreword by Jenae Cohn.
Description: First edition. | Sterling, Virginia : Stylus, 2023. | Includes bibliographical
    references and index. | Summary: "Dispelling the notion that mobile learning is for the
    tech-savvy and adventurous, mobile-mindful teaching offers teachers a way to take a few
    steps at a time, share options with students, and progressively develop ideas and practices.
    The book invites you to explore your own way into mobile learning"-- Provided by
    publisher.
Identifiers: LCCN 2022062262 (print) | LCCN 2022062263 (ebook) | ISBN
    9781642673968 (cloth) | ISBN 9781642673975 (paperback) | ISBN 9781642673982
    (pdf) | ISBN 9781642673999 (epub)
Subjects: LCSH: Mobile communication systems in education. | Web-based instruction.
Classification: LCC LB1044.84 .M66 2023 (print) | LCC LB1044.84 (ebook) | DDC
    371.33--dc23/eng/20230215
LC record available at https://lccn.loc.gov/2022062262
LC ebook record available at https://lccn.loc.gov/2022062263

13-digit ISBN: 978-1-64267-396-8 (cloth)
13-digit ISBN: 978-1-64267-397-5 (paperback)
13-digit ISBN: 978-1-64267-398-2 (library networkable e-edition)
13-digit ISBN: 978-1-64267-399-9 (consumer e-edition)

Printed in the United States of America

All first editions printed on acid free paper that meets the American National Standards
Institute Z39-48 Standard.

Bulk Purchases

Quantity discounts are available for use in workshops and for staff development.

Call 1-800-232-0223

First Edition, 2023

CONTENTS

FOREWORD   vii
  Jenae Cohn

ACKNOWLEDGMENTS   xi

INTRODUCTION   1

1 WHAT MOBILE-MINDFUL LEARNING IS, AND WHY IT MATTERS   6

PART ONE: HOW TO BE A MOBILE-MINDFUL LEARNER

2 START WITH SELF   23

3 MOBILE LEARNING BASIC SKILLS AND CONTENT   31

4 ORGANIZING AND PLANNING MOBILE LEARNING   51

PART TWO: TOWARD MOBILE-MINDFUL TEACHING

5 PREPARE COURSES FOR MOBILE LEARNING   73

6 PREPARE STUDENTS FOR MOBILE LEARNING   92

7 SOCIAL LEARNING AS A MOBILE-MINDFUL CLASS   97

8 DIVE INTO MOBILE-FIRST OPPORTUNITIES   104

PART THREE: MOBILE-MINDFUL ACTIVITIES

9   CASE STUDIES IN MOBILE-MINDFUL TEACHING   115

10   COURSE PLANNING ACTIVITIES   122

11   TEACHING AND LEARNING ACTIVITIES   137

CONCLUSION   159

APPENDIX A: FLUID LEARNING ANALYSIS OF YOUR COURSE   161

APPENDIX B: RECOMMENDED APPS   165

ABOUT THE AUTHOR   169

INDEX   171

FOREWORD

Learning on a mobile device is not the future. It's the present. Students are already using mobile devices for everything from Web browsing to note-taking, navigating the learning management system (LMS), and even writing full term papers (Gikas & Grant, 2013; Roberts & Rees, 2014; Santos et al., 2018; Shyshkanova et al., 2017; Sung & Mayer, 2012). Mobile devices shape how we navigate civic, social, and, yes, educational life worldwide. Yet mobile devices remain a poorly integrated part of the classroom environment. As Helen Crompton and Diane Burke (2018) note in their literature review of mobile learning uses in higher education, very few studies actually explore *how* mobile devices are used as a teaching tool aside from specific project-based contexts such as in producing podcasts or live streaming lecture-based content. Mobile devices have been nearly ubiquitous pieces of consumer technologies for almost two decades now. It's not that we should be using mobile devices just because they're there (and spoiler alert: that's not at all what this book will suggest either!). Rather, it's worth understanding the concerns that undergird the slow pace of adoption to mobile learning. Only then can we be ready to fully embrace the mobile-mindful learning that this book describes.

Ambivalence about using mobile devices for learning stems from two philosophical perspectives on using technology in pedagogical contexts, which science and technology scholars Edward C. Hamilton and Norm Friesen (2013) describe as "essentialism" and "instrumentalism." An essentialist perspective means that a lot of educators see technology as either having a fixed set of characteristics that make the technology either "good" or "bad." An instrumentalist perspective, on the other hand, means that a lot of educators see technology in a completely neutral way, and that the technology simply provides teachers with a passive set of tools that have no impact on the experience whatsoever.

Teaching with technology decisions can quickly become inaccessible and exclusionary if the technology is viewed in overly enthusiastic ways ("phones will revolutionize learning!"), overly negative ways ("phones will destroy learning!") or completely neutral ways ("it doesn't matter if students use a phone or a stone tablet!"). All of these perspectives are problematic for one core reason: they neglect to take the full diversity of student *contexts* and *experiences* into account.

Mobile devices are used for so many different purposes. Outside of school, mobile devices are how we socialize, shop, exercise, pay bills, get medical advice, do calculations, and so on. Ironically, this wide variety of use cases muddles the possibilities for using a mobile device in classroom practice. The push notification and attention-grabbing ecosystem of how most mobile device apps are designed (i.e., with the same design principles as a casino slot machine) seems to run contrary to the focused, concentrated work that higher education pedagogy typically demands.

There probably isn't anyone who wants to do *all* of their schoolwork with one technology, whether it's paper or digitally-based. Most instructors and students alike know that different tasks will be better handled across different technologies, from a laptop to a textbook (Fife, 2017; Hoseth & McLure, 2012; Mueller et al., 2017; Szeto & Cheng, 2016). Yet ignoring mobile learning as an option is simply ignoring another avenue through which learning *can* happen with the appropriate guidance, framing, and open spirit of curiosity.

This volume moves us beyond overly simplified assumptions about using technology for teaching and learning. Instead, it helps readers explore, understand, and appreciate how different teaching and learning contexts can fundamentally shape the possibilities of using mobile devices for meaningful and authentic learning experiences. It's really the word "mindful" in this book's title that's the ticket here. Using a mobile device for learning is not just about what you're using, but *how* and *why* you're using it. This book reminds us that learning doesn't just happen in the four static walls of the classroom during a set period of time. The concept of *fluid learning*, woven in throughout this book, emphasizes that students and instructors alike have option for learning so as not to shut down avenues for learning, but so as to open up new possibilities.

With the concrete tips, detailed lesson plans, and actionable ideas in this book, mobile-mindful learning means that instructors can open up even more potential for students to be intentional about how they use the technologies that are a ubiquitous part of their lives for learning. The guidance from this book will allow educators to empower and trust their students to be agential in determining how, where, or when they can learn best.

Jenae Cohn
Executive Director, Center for Teaching and Learning,
University of California, Berkeley

References

Crompton, H., & Burke, D. (2018). The use of mobile learning in higher education: A systematic review. *Computers & Education, 123*, 53–64. https://doi.org/10.1016/j.compedu.2018.04.007

Fife, J. (2017). Composing focus: Shaping temporal, social, media, social media, and attentional environments. *Composition Forum, 35*(1). https://digitalcommons.wku.edu/cgi/viewcontent.cgi?article=1008&context=english_fac_pub

Gikas, J., & Grant, M. M. (2013). Mobile computing devices in higher education: Student perspectives on learning with cellphones, smartphones & social media. *The Internet and Higher Education, 19*, 18–26. https://doi.org/10.1016/j.iheduc.2013.06.002

Hamilton, E., & Friesen, N. (2013). Online education: A science and technology studies perspective / Éducation en ligne: Perspective des études en science et technologie. *Canadian Journal of Learning and Technology / La Revue Canadienne de l'apprentissage et de La Technologie, 39*(2). https://www.learntechlib.org/p/54417/

Hoseth, A., & McLure, M. (2012). Perspectives on e-books from instructors and students in the social sciences. *Reference & User Services Quarterly, 51*(3), 278–288.

Mueller, K. L., Hanson, M., Martinez, M., & Meyer, L. (2017). Patron preferences: Recreational reading in an academic library. *The Journal of Academic Librarianship, 43*, 72–81. https://doi.org/ 10.1016/j.acalib.2016.08.019

Roberts, N., & Rees, M. (2014). Student use of mobile devices in university lectures. *Australasian Journal of Educational Technology, 30*(4), 415–426. https://doi.org/10.14742/ajet.589

Santos, I. M., Bocheco, O., & Habak, C. (2018). A survey of student and instructor perceptions of personal mobile technology usage and policies for the classroom. *Education and Information Technologies, 23*(2), 617–632. https://doi.org/10.1007/s10639-017-9625-y

Shyshkanova, G., Zaytseva, T., & Frydman, O. (2017). Mobile technologies make education a part of everyday life. *Information and Learning Science, 118*(11/12), 570–582. https://doi.org/10.1108/ILS-03-2017-0019

Sung, E., & Mayer, R. E. (2012). Students' beliefs about mobile devices vs. desktop computers in South Korea and the United States. *Computers & Education, 59*(4), 1328–1338. https://doi.org/10.1016/j.compedu.2012.05.005

Szeto, E., & Cheng, A. Y. N. (2016). Towards a framework of interactions in a blended synchronous learning environment: What effects are there on students' social presence experience? *Interactive Learning Environments, 24*(3), 487–503. https://doi.org/10.1080/10494820.2014.881391

ACKNOWLEDGMENTS

We are the company we keep, from social media to those with whom we share our lives. The seeds of this book were cultivated with brilliant educators I have met at conferences, on Twitter and LinkedIn, and in smaller online communities. Thanks to all who have supported me in this process with wisdom and encouragement through phone calls, messages, and video chats. I am grateful to my many colleagues at Oakland University who talked with me about their teaching, shared syllabi and other aspects of their teaching, and provided the support and enthusiasm that kept me going. Their talent and care are clear in these pages. During the 9 years I worked with my teaching and learning center director, Judy Ableser, she always believed a book was in my future, and I was proud to print a copy of the first completed draft for her on her last day in the office. My husband Shaun Moore, the director of e-Learning at Oakland University, presented at a conference with me on mobile learning in February 2020. Little did we know that we would *really* be stuck with each other in the many months to come as the COVID-19 pandemic hit in earnest mere weeks later. He supported my dissertation and book writing work during the last 2 years, and was a fantastic book reviewer. Shaun, it's your turn to write the next book.

INTRODUCTION

This book started on a phone. In spring 2020, my family was in lockdown due to the worst days of the COVID-19 pandemic. We drove so little then that letting my young kids play in the parked minivan became a favorite activity. In the driver's seat one day, I read through teaching and learning articles in a curation app and took related notes in a different app. I used voice-to-text to take more extensive notes, which was the basis of a teaching resource I wrote for work later that day. Later during brief periods of downtime in meal prep, I remembered I had saved a webinar recording about microlectures and watched it on my phone. I could get the visual input but also followed along with the audio when I had to step away to keep dinner moving.

Leveraging those small learning moments was crucial in that disrupted time. I dearly missed longer and more frequent periods of uninterrupted work time, but having mobile options for learning helped me widen the breadth of my work so that when I had those precious few long work periods, I could focus faster with more resources at my disposal and groundwork set. That summer, I wrote up these reflections and connected them with past readings and newer research on the unmet potential of mobile learning. Despite my general reluctance to be on a smartphone more than I had to, I recognized a need to take mobile learning seriously. EDUCAUSE published my short piece sounding the call for us to embrace mobile learning along with eight ways to increase mobile learning options (Moore, 2020).

I was surprised to hear with how many people this short piece resonated, as I figured "mobile learning" was still a taboo term in higher education. Like so many things related to the pandemic, we were forced to recognize long-standing issues and missed opportunities in education, one of which is taking advantage of "the world changing invention of computers that can and do go everywhere" (Miller, 2022, p. 207). In her book on memory and learning in "a wired world," cognitive psychologist Michelle Miller (2022) addressed the ambivalence we feel about mobile devices in learning. She recognized what I have seen in the literature on mobile learning in higher education: "We're still not quite sure where mobile devices fit into our mission and agenda" (p. 207). Despite an ambivalence she expressed about the phones that so often divert the attention needed for memory and learning, Miller recognized a need to harness "the extraordinary power of mobile devices to our own purposes: accelerating learning and creating avenues to learning for more people throughout the world" (p. 207). More educators than ever agree with this charge, which is likely why you are reading a book on mobile-mindful learning. In this book I hope you find starting points in mobile learning to help keep your students engaged and open up to them as many ways to learn as possible.

Admittedly, I never expected to write a book on mobile learning, but this experience complements others that have come before it. I wasn't drawn to teaching online, but in doing so I found my online classes opened doors to more diverse students than my on-campus classes. From that point I was led to how technology can increase our access to learning, from my work in virtual teaching development to my research on teaching development in social online spaces. My experiences as an instructor, educational developer, writer, researcher, student, parent, and overall lifelong learner inform this mobile-mindful work.

This book is evidence that big ideas can have small, smartphone-sized beginnings.

How This Book Works

This book is for instructors, instructional designers, academic technologists, and anyone who believes in making more learning options available wherever we are, focusing on phones but also in the spirit of capturing learning wherever it may happen. While this book will be useful to educators with a range of technology literacy, I wrote it cognizant that a turn toward more mobile-mindful options is a significant pedagogical shift for most. Therefore, the first section of the book addresses why we should all be mobile-mindful even if we are a little skeptical of how much course work should happen on a smartphone. After this argument for making more learning accessible on phones, we will explore some mobile learning basics in the How to Be a Mobile-Mindful Learner section. We will "start with self"—to identify and evaluate how our work and learning move across devices and what advantages and barriers we encounter along the way. We will also try mobile-mindful learning moves firsthand, such as how to engage in different types of learning (digital reading, audio and visual learning, and social learning), curate our learning to work across multiple devices and contexts, and regulate our learning through time and task management process and tools.

Once we have learned mobile learning basics experientially, we can shift "Toward Mobile-Mindful Teaching," taking what we have learned to make more learning actions available on phones and show students the way. We will start with ways to add mobile options to existing learning materials and activities, from neutral formats to exploring how learning management systems (LMS) function on a phone. Ethical considerations should also be a part of mobile-mindful course planning, such as student access to devices and internet, privacy, and potential taxes on attention. From there, we will plan how to start increasing mobile learning options such as gathering timely feedback from students during class; sharing learning in social, collaborative spaces; increasing granular, self-paced learning materials; offering multimodal assessment options; and even encouraging students to create mobile-friendly materials.

To help implement mobile-mindful teaching, this book offers two groups of activities you can use directly or tweak for your needs. Course Planning Activities will help prepare a more mobile-mindful course such as evaluating and analyzing the current accessibility of your course, creating a mobile-mindful syllabus, facilitating class communications, and planning core mobile learning activities. Once courses are planned for mobile-mindful learning, the Teaching and Learning Activities chapter provides mobile activities you could do with your students such as assembling a mobile learning app kit, sending "did you know" syllabus-based reminders, facilitating a class "slow chat," and inviting students to embrace mobile-friendly presentations, research, and applications in their fields of study.

When exploring significant pedagogical shifts, practical bite-size ideas can help us try something new right away. Therefore, you will notice examples, case studies, tips, and app highlights throughout the book. To embody adding mobile-mindful options to print and digital reading, you will also be prompted with QR codes to explore something on your phone while reading the book, such as self-assessment forms, tools, and other materials that are best experienced on a phone. The Recommended Apps section includes apps I referred to throughout the book, plus additional apps that may support the mobile-mindful learning moves addressed in this book.

To avoid crowding this book, you can find more mobile-mindful teaching ideas and supplementary resources at christinamoorephd.com/ MobileMindful. I am sure you have plenty of stories, experiences, questions, ideas, and resources to share related to mobile-mindful teaching: Please share them on my Mobile-Mindful Teaching and Learning website so that I can feature them in blog posts.

What This Book Is Not

When it comes to mobile learning, many think of "mobile-first" design and making every course action available from a phone. Some institutions and individuals are pursuing such possibilities, and microlearning endeavors in corporate learning circles are diving into mobile-first programs. While I am intrigued by those exploring fully mobile-accessible programs such as Los Angeles Pacific University (Supiano, 2021) and we can learn a lot from such efforts, this book prioritizes intentionally fitting mobile learning into an overall fluid learning environment in which students have learning options across devices and learning situations. This book resists forcing students to do work on their phones, but invites them to explore how to better use their phones for learning.

This book will provide recommendations on apps and tools, but it will not be a deep dive into technical capabilities. It is meant for an audience across all tech levels, especially those who feel they need some preparation and support to begin thinking about adding mobile learning options to their courses. The main motivation for mobile learning in this book is to increase learning access, so it places pedagogy before educational technology. Educators should not feel that adding apps and tools automatically results in better student experiences: Of 2,798 undergraduate students surveyed, more than a quarter felt they were being assigned too many different learning tools (Read, 2022). This book's app recommendations will not be comprehensive and instead favor apps that students will find familiar and will be able to work with across other devices. The book also will not dive deep into mobile capabilities like virtual or augmented reality. That being said, I hope readers will build on this book's ideas to explore VR and other innovative ways to engage in mobile teaching and learning. I also hope you will call on instructional designers and academic technologists to support you in implementing mobile-mindful learning options.

This book is a call to be curious about what mobile learning could offer, even if with some skepticism in tow. If we care about learning, it is difficult to ignore what is possible when students can access learning more often on a phone, especially when we know that they would not only use these opportunities but welcome them. Instructors who have found that teaching online has helped them improve their overall teaching practices will find the same result in thinking about facilitating more frequent, granular, and connected ways to learn. Nevertheless, I acknowledge that mobile-mindful learning may feel like a leap, so it is worth laying out the rationale and priorities for being mobile-mindful educators.

References

Miller, M. D. (2022). *Remembering and forgetting in the age of technology: Teaching, learning, and the science of memory in a wired world.* West Virginia Press.

Moore, C. (2020, June 22). Now is the time to embrace mobile learning. *EDUCAUSE Review.* https://er.educause.edu/blogs/2020/6/now-is-the-time-to-embrace-mobile-learning

Read, D. L. (2022, February 9). Top Hat field report: 2,798 students on assessments, career-readiness, and diversity and inclusion in the classroom. *Top Hat Blog.* https://tophat.com/blog/feb-2022-student-survey/

Supiano, B. (2021, February 25). Teaching: Lessons from one university's fully mobile courses. *Chronicle of Higher Education.* https://www.chronicle.com/newsletter/teaching/2021-02-25

I

WHAT MOBILE-MINDFUL LEARNING IS, AND WHY IT MATTERS

In the early 2000s, I remember seeing commercials introducing a new feature on cellphones: text messaging. I don't remember the details of the commercials, just younger people smiling at very short messages on their cellphones. I didn't get it. I remember how silly and useless it seemed, wondering why people would use T9 Word on a cellphone pad to type out short messages when they could just call. I couldn't imagine having a full conversation through text messages. Fifteen years later, a colleague who is older than me said she felt it was entirely too intimate to have someone's voice in her ear, that the only person she had a voice call with was her mother.

While our everyday norms around phone use have changed drastically in the last 20 years, education norms around phone use have barely nudged. While smartphone use and ownership are very high around the world and only increasing, its use for learning in higher education is still minimal. Embedding mobile learning into pedagogy may be the most crucial factor in student smartphone use for education and learning (Hao et al., 2017). Since 2012, University of Central Florida's Center for Distributed Learning has taken on this challenge by increasing mobile learning and app options specifically for UCF students, including working with faculty to implement more mobile learning options into courses. In their 2016 survey (n=1680), 45% of students said professors asked students to use mobile apps for their learning as compared to 88% of students being prompted to use laptops (Seilhamer et al., 2018). These mobile learning numbers are higher than the average higher education institution, as UCF's numbers reflect more than 6 years of institutional resources dedicated to increasing mobile learning.

6

It is not enough for students to simply own mobile tech or for materials to be available on mobile phones: It is when instructors mindfully implement mobile learning opportunities that students see the usefulness of learning via phone. Plenty of individual instructors seize the opportunity to use mobile devices for place-based learning, primary research, and other projects, but such mobile pedagogy still comprises few faculty overall. More instructors may see the use of smartphones as audience response systems, but little else. In short, faculty attitudes about mobile tech in the classroom continue to be "slow to change" (Gierdowski, 2019). Mobile learning is not a common consideration in most of our courses because of some ideas we hold such as the following.

Criticism 1: Phones Are the Enemy of Attention in Our Classrooms (and Elsewhere)

Phones produce in us a deep dread, loathing the inevitability of how much our eyes are on them. Digital researcher danah boyd (2014) has found that while parents lament their teens' use of phones, these teens complain just as much about their parents being glued to their phones. Most of us don't like that we are on our phone all of the time, and yet we accept we cannot compete with the distraction it offers. Like the theaters do right before a movie starts, we try to ask students to not use their phones during our classes, asking them to hold their attention in this space of learning, for learning cannot happen without attention (Lang, 2020).

Criticism 1 Reframed: What if the source of our loathing was not necessarily being on our phone, but being on our phone *mindlessly*? We don't feel the same self-loathing when we are on our phone catching up with a dear friend, reading a great article in the waiting room, or listening to an engrossing podcast. The ideal flow of mobile learning is in granting phones our attention only when we want to and in an intentional way. Instead of phones directing attention away from meaningful learning experiences, it can instead bring attention toward them more frequently.

Criticism 2: Phones Reduce Rather Than Expand Learning

The call for more mobile learning opportunities might make us picture students reading and writing less, education surrendering to smaller screens and shorter attention spans. Will the academic paper be reduced to tweets? Will books be exchanged for apps? Mobile learning seems antithetical to the type of deep, critical thinking in which we seek to engage our students. The desire to turn everything into a TED Talk comes at the risk of oversimplification in a learning environment that values complication and complexity.

Criticism 2 Reframed: What if mobile learning opportunities provided the cognitive links that build toward complexity and critical thinking? When our students are novices in our disciplines, they might flounder as they try to make sense of basics and advanced concepts simultaneously. By teaching students how mobile-mindful learning can help them capture their thoughts and connections, they will be better prepared when they have the opportunity to engage in larger, more challenging learning activities. Shorter, valuable recall and synthesis exercises such as flashcards and summaries precede smartphones, but mobile learning can greatly increase frequent, granular learning actions that lay the foundation for big-picture thinking.

Criticism 3: Phones Are Not Compatible With Our Learning Activities

Our learning materials and actions are simply not designed for phones. Considering how every learning activity can be scaled to a phone is not just a matter of format, but of completely rethinking learning activities.

Criticism 3 Reframed: What if our activities are more compatible than we think? Some of our reading assignments and other activities may already be mobile-accessible, and others may only require minimal format adjustment. For actions that may require more labor and rethinking, starting small may open up more possibilities than imagined. We have had similar criticisms about teaching online and in other modality changes, only to find that our overall teaching improved by expanding our teaching design. By recognizing current and future opportunities, we can find both compatibility and new possibilities.

This book will acknowledge these and other skeptical thoughts more deeply and engage in productive reframing of intentional, meaningful teaching opportunities. For too long, mobile learning has intimidated instructors who consider it something reserved for the most tech-savvy and tech-adventurous. Instead, mobile-*mindful* teaching is about creating fluid learning opportunities and rich learning ecologies, both of which propose continuity in learning across devices and within diverse environments. By taking feasible steps toward considering mobile learning possibilities in teaching choices, any instructor can be mobile-mindful in a way that vastly increases student access to learning.

Mere decades ago, educators had the same reluctance about our students and ourselves using machines for our lofty learning purposes. In 1999, composition studies scholar Cynthia Selfe called out her computer-averse professional organization for "not paying attention" to the influence of computers on literacy education. Back then it was computers that produced in instructors "a kind of cultural strangeness that is off-putting"; now it is mobile learning. The argument made then fits well with our current attitudes and opportunities with mobile learning: We need to think about mobile learning not as "helping students work effectively with communication software and hardware, but, rather, also a matter of helping them to understand and be able to assess—to pay attention to—the social, economic, and pedagogical implications of new communication technologies and technological initiatives that affect their lives" (p. 432). We do not have to shy away from the negative effects smartphones have on our lives in order to explore the positive effects they could and already do have on learning.

This book focuses on increasing our mobile learning curiosity, starting with ourselves as mobile learners rather than mere mobile consumers. Then, we will explore how we can encourage students to be mobile learners by not only making more course material available on a phone, but also guiding them toward expanding mobile learning into all of their available learning options and being savvier learners and thinkers. No matter your level of techiness, this book is about connecting learning opportunities to mobile phones so that students have easier, more frequent access to course learning.

Defining Mobile-Mindful Learning

Mobile learning generally refers to learning that can be facilitated through a mobile device, most often referring to a smartphone for its mobility, ubiquity, and capability. While tablets and laptops are a part of the mobile learning landscape, they are not as portable and widely used as smartphones (Seilhamer et al., 2018). For this reason, much of this book will focus on how we can make learning more accessible on phones. However, I encourage thinking of mobile learning in much broader terms. As described in the concept of "fluid learning" (Fang, 2014), learning becomes mobile in our ability to move learning across space and contexts, meaning a student can strategically translate learning that happened while walking or commuting to learning while sitting in front of a desktop. In other words, we can engage in and extend our learning no matter where we are.

Mobile-mindful learning also recognizes that a body in motion often thinks differently than one sitting in a chair. The importance of learning in motion is receiving needed attention through books such as Susan Hrach's *Minding Bodies: How Physical Space, Sensation, and Movement Affect Learning* and more generally in Annie Murphy Paul's *The Extended Mind: The Power of Thinking Outside of the Brain*. Recognizing learning as mediated through the body also considers sensory experiences such as manipulating objects, noticing scents, and overall how our bodies experience a physical space and how these factors influence our learning. From this perspective, mobile-mindful learning could also increase offline learning, which can use phones to capture and digitize low- and no-tech learning activities.

In short, mobile-mindful learning can be

- engaging on a smartphone
- learning that moves across and away from devices
- capturing experiential, place-based learning with a phone
- learning while in motion

With this broader lens, this book's mobile-mindful learning approach will be different than approaches that focus only on phone-mediated mobile learning or "mobile first" approaches. A mobile-mindful approach does not cram every learning activity into a small screen but recognizes the learning that is already occurring on phones and how much more we could accomplish. These mobile-mindful learning definitions and considerations are developed throughout the book.

Key Frameworks to Mobile-Mindful Learning: Universal Design for Learning, Fluid Learning, and Learning Ecologies

We tend to view only a couple of contexts as useful for academic learning: in the classroom and formal homework periods in quiet places such as the library or our home (if we are so lucky to have distraction-free home spaces). When our instructional design limits learning to these realms, we miss out on all of the learning spaces in between. In truth, we are learning all of the time, and we want to learn more often. Three frameworks can help us see how mobile-mindful learning can fit into a larger learning landscape: universal design for learning, fluid learning, and learning ecologies.

Universal design for learning (UDL) is a key framework for considering mobile-mindful learning. In line with fluid learning, UDL is a brain-based framework that connects learning design with the variable ways humans learn. Based on how the brain works in learning activities, a leading organization called CAST (n.d.) organized UDL in three principles: providing multiple means of engagement (motivation and involvement of the learner), representation (how concepts are presented to learners), and action and expression (how learning is demonstrated). In a UDL mindset, mobile-mindful teaching is not about forcing people to learn on phones but using phones as a way to increase access to all types of learning, even offline learning. Thomas Tobin and Kirsten Behling's *Reach Everyone, Teach Everyone: Universal Design for Learning in Higher Education* (2018) includes the chapter "Meet the Mobile

Learners," where they argued that in order to implement UDL, one has to be more mindful of mobile learning. In many ways, reading this book chapter pointed me in the direction of mobile-mindful learning and introduced me to the next key framework: fluid learning.

Fluid learning seeks to provide continuity in learning among mobile and nonmobile devices (Fang, 2014). Fluid learning means students can access learning material or activities on whatever technology they want at any time. Fluid learning is defined by five characteristics:

- neutrality: works well on any device
- granularity: can be consumed in smaller units
- portability: used across platforms
- interactivity: potential connection among others
- ubiquity: learning beyond devices, existing everywhere

These principles will be applied throughout the book, but all of these qualities promote a more universal design instead of a mobile-specific design.

Learning ecologies is a framework for analyzing how environments cultivate three types of learning: formal (learning institutions like schools), nonformal (organized, but not with accreditation), and informal (spontaneous, unplanned; Barron, 2006). While fluid learning attends to the flow of learning based on device, learning ecologies attend to the flow of learning based on context and formality. Learning ecologies consider how these three types of learning can be better connected, such as through social media, communication apps, and community partnerships. In teaching educators in graduate level courses, two instructors used the learning ecologies framework to encourage students to develop "learner-generated playgrids" through which students learned how to connect course-related learning to nonformal and informal methods of professional development, such as through social media and public annotation (Hollett & Kalir, 2017).

Mobile-Mindful Learning Terms

These terms have been used to describe how learning can happen with phones. Based on this book's focus on "mobile-mindful" teaching and learning rather than mobile learning alone, some terms will be used more than others.

- *Mobile learning:* Learning that happens on mobile devices, normally referring to a smartphone, but in earlier studies have also referred to portable phones with limited internet and app capabilities. "M-learning" is a shortened term used for mobile learning.

- *Microlearning*: Learning designed in bite-sizes, focusing on the granular component in "fluid learning" (Fang, 2014). This instructional design distills learning content and activities to the smallest amount of content possible that can be easily found and accessed. While microlearning considers the size of learning content more than devices, mobile accessibility is crucial to microlearning. This learning mentality is popular in corporate professional development models, particularly in fields where professionals need skill training immediately as situations arise or need frequent recall practice (Udalova, 2022).
- *"Mobile-first"*: This web design mindset starts with the usability and accessibility of web content on a phone, and then adjusts the design to also accommodate other devices. The mobile-first mentality acknowledges an increased use of mobile phones and that it is easier to design mobile-accessible web content from the outset rather than retroactively adjust web content to be usable on a phone.

Now that we have established what mobile-mindful teaching and learning are and how they differ from traditional mobile learning ideas, let's explore why it is worth our curiosity and consideration. Even if we are not thrilled with how phones tend to operate in our everyday lives and our classrooms, mobile-mindful teaching is not just about increasing access. Mobile-mindful teaching can strengthen all of the other learning students are doing and give more support and space for students to develop ideas and express themselves.

Mobile Learning Increases Access

The only "mobility" to my undergraduate and graduate education was in the novels and notebooks I carried. As an older millennial and commuter student, I typed papers on my home desktop when it worked and otherwise relied on the local library's computer lab. A fellow graduate student who worked in the online learning office took pity on me and helped me pick out a netbook. (We got married 4 years later, following a proposal partially mediated through Moodle, the learning management system.) Smartphones were only for the tech savvy, and I held off getting one until well after my college days.

The poor college student motif plays out differently now: While technology ownership is up for all U.S. demographics, a smartphone is the first and main piece of computer technology any one person in the United States owns. While 85% of Americans own a smartphone, ownership jumps to 96% for those ages 18–29 (Pew Research Center, 2021). Around 15% are smartphone-dependent, meaning the only personal access they have to the internet is through their phone and they lack home broadband internet, and they tend to be younger adults and lower income Americans. While 76% of lower income adults have smartphones, only 57% have broadband at home. When analyzing this data by race, a quarter of Hispanics are "smartphone-only" internet users, whereas rates among white and Black adults are about half of that rate (Atske & Perrin, 2019). University of Central Florida's multiyear study of mobile learning found similar figures in its data from more than 4,000 students: 100% of their students had smartphones, and women and students of color used their phones for learning most often (Seilhamer et al., 2018).

I urge us to frame these stats positively: All demographics have seen increases in computer technology ownership that help us connect to information and people. Since most people across all U.S. demographics have smartphones, instructors have powerful ways of connecting students with learning beyond the classroom and desk. Similarly, smartphone ownership is increasing all over the world. Median smartphone ownership in advanced economies is 76%, with the median in emerging economies at 45%. Furthermore, smartphones are often the only means of internet access, as a much lower percent of people access the internet with a desktop, laptop, or tablet (median 34%; Pew Research Center, 2019). Increasing mobile-mindful learning can prepare college students to work in global markets whose main connection to individuals will be through smartphones.

We may not have guessed these numbers exactly, but they likely aren't surprising. Yet the way our teaching tethers learning to larger devices does not fit with this reality: Instructors are relying on technology for teaching and learning more than ever, but often not in line with the technology that students use most often (Gierdowski, 2019) or that they use in their careers after graduation (Levy & Sidhu, 2013). As mentioned earlier, while 88% of University of Central Florida student respondents' instructors prompted them to use laptops on assignments, only 45% reported the same for smartphone use on assignments. Less than half of instructors are taking advantage of the phones almost every student has, and 82% of these students reported using smartphones on their own for learning (Seilhamer et al., 2018). UCF's study has shown increases in instructor implementation, yet it still greatly lags students' actual use—and this is at an institution heavily invested in increasing mobile learning opportunities.

While more opportunities to learn with and through smartphones most benefit young students, students of color, and low-income students, mobile learning benefits anyone who has limited time and many life demands but still wants to pursue higher education and build lifelong learning habits. UCF's study showed that while there was some consistency in the demographics who use phones for learning more frequently, these results do not pinpoint exact people and groups who benefit from more mobile learning opportunities. For example, while students with grades on the lower end of passing reported using smartphones for learning more than other students, Honors College students used mobile apps for learning more than students from other colleges. Colleges whose students most engaged in mobile learning were from medicine, nursing, and public health (Seilhamer et al., 2018). These results suggest that while material circumstances lead some students to use their phones for learning more often than others, all students benefit from increased opportunities guided by their instructors. Forty percent of students in the UCF survey wanted their instructors to implement mobile learning more often.

Unfortunately, we are working against our normal experience of students using phones to disengage from class sessions. It is difficult to get over this frustration. While the skepticism is not unfounded, we could embrace much needed nuance on how phones affect learning. While some studies have found negative correlations between mobile phone usage and cognitive tasks, most were under very specific circumstances (e.g., secondary school students; mobile multitasking) and could not perfectly set up experimental and control groups (Wilmer et al., 2017).

Taking drastic, sweeping approaches to technology frustrations can increase educational inequities: In EDUCAUSE Center for Analysis and Research's (ECAR) 2018 study, students of color, female students, poor students, and disabled students reported the harm of classroom technology bans on their learning, which would make them unable to access e-versions of course materials: "In some cases, faculty ban or discourage devices in classrooms on the basis of research that simply confirms their biases against those digital devices—that they are distracting, that student device usage implies disrespect or a lack of attention, or that students are not taking good notes. This approach can do real, if unintended, harm" (Galanek et al., 2018, para. 3).

I am not arguing that concerns about phone-related distractibility are overexaggerated, but I argue that mobile learning can be done well under specific conditions, and that we get better results from being mobile-mindful rather than mobile-resistant. Using mobile devices for learning does not have to be all or nothing: As James Lang advocated in his book *Distracted: Why Students Can't Focus and What You Can Do About It* (2020), it is best to consider context and activities in encouraging or discouraging technology use. For activities that require specific attention to here-and-now activities like role-playing and storytelling, perhaps it is warranted to encourage students not to access their phones during those 25 minutes. If students are working in small groups on an activity or have practice time, it seems more appropriate to open up technology use. Phones are great for keeping students connected to classmates and course content when they are not in the classroom; and, admittedly, they are ripe for distraction during live sessions. That being said, I prefer to plan class sessions that prompt the right kind of tech use, such as students working in small groups to complete a series of scaffolded tasks for which I give timely feedback.

It does not take much to reframe our consideration of mobile learning. When we start to see how often our students could be thinking about ideas related to our course, especially with what we know about the brain and learning, we can't help but be intrigued.

Mobile Pedagogy Increases Learning

Consider these questions (preferably writing down your answers).

1. How many hours per week do you think students should dedicate to your course?
2. How many hours per week do you think your students *actually* dedicate to your course?

Admittedly, this is an overly simplistic measurement of how students learn in a course, but such consideration can help us tease out learning expectations and behaviors. I don't think any of us have the same answer for both No. 1 and No. 2, and we probably all wish students spent more time learning for our course. While students often are recommended to spend 2 hours on schoolwork for every 1 hour spent in the classroom, they are on average doing half that (McCormick, 2011). We may try to address this discrepancy by writing in the syllabus the institution's guidance on time they should dedicate per credit hour, paring down our reading and course activities or sticking to our standards even if it causes us disappointment and prompts students to cram. No matter how we explain the time discrepancy—students are too busy, students are distracted, our expectations need to change—the discrepancy persists.

What if the issue is not the amount of time, but how that time is distributed?

What does learning look like when students leave the classroom? If pressed, we might picture students sitting down for at least an hour multiple times a week. If we pictured what students are actually doing, it might be something closer to cramming, spending hours before a class session doing everything they were supposed to do over the past week. Such a pace leaves little room for curiosity, exploration, and overall idea development. Part of the issue might be a lack of opportunity to engage in course content during the 30 minutes in the waiting room, the 45 minutes on a commute, the extra 15 minutes waiting for a friend, even the 8 minutes waiting in line at a store. Students with disabilities are more likely to be in such situations attending disability-related appointments (Robson, 2019). The barrier is not necessarily time, but access.

If all course learning has to be done with bulky materials and long stretches of time, students can only effectively think about their courses a fraction of the time. Mobile learning could be a key way to achieve the type of breadth (i.e., coverage) we struggle to achieve, and it could also be a way to deepen learning through frequent, varied retrieval. In other words, mobile-mindful teaching and learning not only make it more likely students will "do the reading," but also that they will think about the reading more frequently, over longer periods of time, and in different contexts.

Mobile Learning Increases Quality Learning

Increasing access is not just about convenience, but about improved learning. In the popular Learning How to Learn Coursera MOOC, Barbara Oakley (n.d.) explained important brain processes in learning, such as chunking, distributed practice and spaced repetition, and focused and diffuse modes of thinking. Mobile learning is key to all of these learning mechanisms: Learning made into smaller units fits "chunking," mobile flashcards and quizzes allow for more frequent practice, and more frequent practice allows course content to employ our focused and diffuse modes of thinking. (Focused mode refers to direct attention to a task while diffuse mode recognizes how our brain works on a problem in the background.)

To this effect, Oakley replaced the phrase "practice makes perfect" with "practice makes permanent" to emphasize that if we want to really remember something, we must practice frequently. She likened the process to laying bricks: It has to be done one layer at a time with periods of rest to allow the mortar to harden. Oakley continuously called for increased retrieval practice as an important part of learning. Likewise, cognitive psychologist Michelle D. Miller (2022) argued that memorization is important for learning, as our brain has to quickly and independently recall information in order to effectively engage in higher order thinking tasks. We might encourage students to engage in these frequent learning approaches, but if all of our course learning materials live in large books or PDFs in the LMS, it is difficult for students to know how to access learning in smaller but more frequent processes. Flashcards might be the only familiar strategy for students when smartphones can provide many more types of learning opportunities.

In short, more opportunities to learn on a phone not only increase opportunities to learn, but create better learning opportunities, especially in training our brains in the repetitious work that supports more complex and time-consuming tasks like writing a paper and projects. It is like practicing a sport: By learning many different moves and exercising in many ways, the body prepares itself to engage in a physically and mentally rigorous game and is able to improvise and adapt in any situation. Ideally when a mobile-mindful learner sits down to solve a complex problem, write a paper, or prepare a presentation, they have practiced core concepts that require less mental bandwidth and they have already recorded some ideas ahead of time. During class discussions, students will be able to make connections between different theories or scenarios if they have reviewed theories frequently and read several short scenarios that are easy to find and view on their phones. Making our course activities more accessible on a phone and explicitly teaching students how to be mobile learners can increase students' learning breadth and depth. Shifting to more frequent, smaller scale learning activities engages students in the type of habitual mental activity that increases productivity and creativity (Duhigg, 2016; Levintin, 2015). In the How to Be a Mobile-Mindful Learner section, you can "start with self" and see how setting learning goals and creating intentional, persistent, and granular mobile learning habits can reap significant learning benefits.

Mobile-Mindful Learning: Beyond Phone Screens

Officially, mobile learning is focused on learning via smartphone. I prefer to explore "mobile-mindful" learning for two reasons: to promote a nonintimidating approach to increasing mobile learning opportunities and to avoid forcing mobile learning on students. While the vast majority of students attending U.S. higher education institutions have smartphones, we cannot assume every one of our students has one or has equal access to signal bandwidth or that everyone is comfortable using a small touch screen. Students may struggle to learn on phones for a variety of reasons. Even mobile learning experts acknowledge that we cannot expect every type of educational activity will be fully accessible to every learner, which is why we should design "multiple ways for students to engage with the learning" (Robson, 2019, p. 550) as supported by UDL.

While we need to focus on phones since they are ubiquitous and underutilized, it is most beneficial to think of how mobile learning fits in with other types of learning. To get the most out of mobile-mindful learning, we should design learning opportunities that thrive on phones, but allow students' phone-based learning activity to support learning elsewhere, and vice versa. Throughout the book, we will include mobile-mindful learning strategies that help us draw our attention away from screens while still using phones to capture activity such as through creating video and audio content, using voice dictation, taking photos, and other ways to engage in and demonstrate learning.

Mobile Learning Is Learning in Motion

The "mobile" in "mobile learning" considers how we can access learning content wherever we go. In other words, a set body of knowledge stays the same whether we are studying at the library, sitting at the kitchen table, or riding the bus. While this can be true, in it lies the temptation to think of learning as place-neutral and best executed with a still body. The closer we look at mobile learning and align it with how humans actually learn, the more we see the need for place and motion in mobile-mindful teaching and learning.

While neuroscience and learning research are not yet abundant enough to validate some movement-based learning ideas such as cross-lateral movement and "neurobics," it is clear that we are more than a "brain on a stick" (Hrach, 2021, p. xiv). We learn through and with our bodies, even using the body to think outside of our brain (Paul, 2021). Mobile-mindful learning acknowledges how learning happens through our senses, places, and experiences, and smartphones in particular can help capture and curate such learning. To counteract the dread we might feel about mobile learning drawing us into ever-smaller screens, mobile learning could untether us from a placelessness embedded in many course learning processes. Throughout this book, we will explore how phones can increase place-conscious and movement-enabled learning.

What Now?

So far I hope your interest in mobile-mindful learning is at least piqued. We can see that there are significant learning gains to be made by at least making more of our current content easier to access on phones, especially for those who need this access the most. Learning gains come not only in quantity, but also in quality. If mobile-mindful courses mean students are accessing content more frequently, they are gaining cognitive benefits both when they are directly engaged in learning (focused mode) and when they are not (diffuse mode). More students will "do the reading" and have examples and connections to talk about.

We can further explore mobile-mindful learning even while feeling the *ugh* of phones in general. "Mobile-mindful" is not just being cognizant of mobile access to our course content, but also being mindful about how we are using our phones. We can be mobile-mindful teachers without unleashing all attention on small screens. Mobile-mindfulness may just free us from screens in general, allowing us to capture print, material, motion, and other media and forms of expression beyond typing. Within the lenses of learning ecologies, fluid learning, and UDL, mobile-mindful learning forges a continuity that is critical to learning.

References

Atske, S., & Perrin, A. (2019, July 16). *Home broadband adoption, computer ownership vary by race, ethnicity in the U.S.* Pew Research Center. https://www.pewresearch.org/fact-tank/2021/07/16/home-broadband-adoption-computer-ownership-vary-by-race-ethnicity-in-the-u-s/

Barron, B. (2006). Interest and self-sustained learning as catalysts of development: A learning ecologies perspective. *Human Development, 49*(4), 193–224. https://www.jstor.org/stable/26763888

boyd, d. (2014). *It's complicated: The social lives of networked teens.* Yale University Press. https://www.danah.org/books/ItsComplicated.pdf

CAST. (n.d.). *About universal design for learning.* https://www.cast.org/impact/universal-design-for-learning-udl

Duhigg, C. (2016). *Smarter faster better: The transformative power of real productivity.* Random House.

Fang, B. (2014, October 13). Creating a fluid learning environment. *EDUCAUSE Review.* https://er.educause.edu/articles/2014/10/creating-a-fluid-learning-environment

Galanek, J. D., Gierdowski, D. C., & Brooks, D. C. (2018, October). *ECAR study of undergraduate students and information technology, 2018.* https://www.educause.edu/ecar/research-publications/ecar-study-of-undergraduate-students-and-information-technology/2018/device-use-and-importance

Gierdowski, D. C. (2019, October). *ECAR study of undergraduate students and information technology, 2019.* https://library.educause.edu/resources/2019/10/2019-study-of-undergraduate-students-and-information-technology

Hao, S., Dennen, V. P., & Mei, L. (2017). Influential factors for mobile learning acceptance among Chinese users. *Educational Technology Research and Development, 65*(1), 101–123. https://doi.org/10.1007/s11423-016-9465-2

Hollett, T., & Kalir, J. H. (2017). Mapping playgrids for learning across space, time, and scale. *TechTrends, 61*, 236–245. https://doi.org/10.1007/s11528-016-0138-0

Hrach, S. (2021). *Minding bodies: How physical space, sensation, and movement affect learning.* West Virginia University Press.

Lang, J. (2020). *Distracted: Why students can't focus and what you can do about it.* Basic Books.

Levintin, D. L. (2015). *The organized mind: Thinking straight in the age of information overload.* Dutton.

Levy, J., & Sidhu, P. (2013). In the U.S., 21st-century skills linked to work success; real-world problem-solving most strongly tied to work quality. *Gallup Poll News Service.* http://www.gallup.com

McCormick, A. C. (2011). It's about time: What to make of reported declines in how much college students study. *Liberal Education, 97*(1). https://www.aacu.org

Miller, M. D. (2022). *Remembering and forgetting in the age of technology: Teaching, learning, and the science of memory in a wired world.* West Virginia Press.

Oakley, B., & Sejnowski, T. (n.d.). *Learning how to learn: Powerful mental tools to help you master tough subjects.* Coursera. https://www.coursera.org/learn/learning-how-to-learn

Paul, A. M. (2021). *The extended mind: The power of thinking outside the brain.* Mariner Books.

Pew Research Center. (2019, November 20). *Mobile divides in emerging economies.* www.pewresearch.org/internet/2019/11/20/mobile-divides-in-emerging-economies/

Pew Research Center. (2021, April 17). *Mobile facts sheet (2021).* pewresearch.org/internet/fact-sheet/mobile/

Robson, L. (2019). Accessibility challenges in mobile learning. In Y. A. Zhang & D. Cristol (Eds.), *Handbook of mobile teaching and learning* (pp. 549–564). Springer Nature Singapore. https://doi.org/10.1007/978-981-13-2766-7_39

Seilhamer, R., Chen, B., deNoyelles, A., Raible, J., Bauer, J., & Salter, A. (2018). 2018 mobile survey report. *UCF Center for Distributed Learning: University of Central Florida.* https://digitallearning.ucf.edu/msi/research/mobile/survey2018/

Selfe, C. L. (1999). Technology and literacy: A story about the perils of not paying attention. *College Composition and Communication, 50*(3), 411–436. https://doi.org/10.2307/358859

Tobin, T., & Behling, K. T. (2018). Meet the mobile learners. *Reach everyone, teach everyone: Universal design for learning in higher education.* Western Virginia University Press.

Udalova, K. (2022, March 3). 4 microlearning examples you can use now to improve training content. *7taps Blog.* https://www.7taps.com/blog/4-microlearning-examples-you-can-use-now-to-improve-training-content

Wilmer, H. H., Sherman, L. E., & Chein, J. M. (2017). Smartphones and cognition: A review of research exploring the links between mobile technology habits and cognitive functioning. *Frontiers in Psychology.* https://doi.org/10.3389/fpsyg.2017.00605

PART ONE

HOW TO BE A MOBILE-MINDFUL LEARNER

2

START WITH SELF

With the *why* of mobile-mindful learning established, let's turn to the *how*. If we intend to facilitate mobile-mindful learning opportunities for students, we will need to have firsthand experience at being mobile-mindful learners. Tobin and Behling (2018) defined mobile learners as those "who use mobile technology on a daily basis for problem solving, information gathering, and social purposes—regardless of their age" (p. 79). To get to know what a mobile learner is and can be, it is crucial to start with ourselves, as "our own experiences can provide us with a guide to the use of mobile devices in learning," from the resources we consult most often to the technology barriers we encounter (Hokanson, 2014, p. 53). At the very least, we as educators should be "paying attention" to how technology affordances affect our students' learning opportunities (Selfe, 1999).

In discussing her book *Small Teaching Online*, Flower Darby argued that many instructors struggle to teach well online because they likely have limited online learning experiences, if any. While a lifetime of learning and teaching in brick-and-mortar classrooms gives us some idea of what contributes to a positive or negative learning environment, we may have zero to few online learning experiences to draw from when it comes to teaching online (Stachowiak, 2019). That lack of exposure and challenge is greatly increased when it comes to mobile learning, which is why I propose a "start with self" model. Doing so will not only diversify your learning ecologies but inspire mobile learning options for your courses and students. "Starting with self" can also help you find out firsthand what works and what does not work, so you know how students will experience it.

This section introduces how to be mobile-mindful in our personal learning opportunities, introducing common learning actions and how they are best situated on a phone. We will explore learning from a variety of text formats, including digital reading and multimodal learning as well as learning from others with social online spaces. Then we will practice organizing all of this in mobile curation processes from initial collection to application and dissemination. We will plan mobile-mindful methods for reaching learning goals including flashcards, task lists, and managing nudges and notifications.

With each learning element, you will be able to try these out to boost your personal and professional learning goals and curiosities. You will observe your mobile learning habits, identify opportunities for increased mobile learning, set goals and intentions, and reflect on the result. Throughout this process we will link general learning principles and theories to mobile learning actions. Establishing mobile learning principles and practices here will lay the foundation for how to facilitate mobile-mindful learning opportunities for students. The more you pay attention to your mobile habits and bend them toward intentional learning, the more you will see promising, attainable applications in your teaching and for student learning.

Assess Your Phone Behavior

These items prompt reflection on how often you interact with your phone and in what ways. They are not all necessarily good or bad, but simply ways to acknowledge how you use your phone and whether this behavior is intentional and desired. Check the items that match your phone use in the following list. Alternatively, by scanning the QR code with your phone (see Figure 2.1), you can access a digital version of this list where you can fill out the form, annotate, and save the results. To access a digital version on a computer, go to christinamoorephd.com/MobileMindful.

Figure 2.1. QR code for phone use checklist.

How to Scan a QR Code: A QR code is an image that allows a phone to capture a URL and navigate to a website without typing in a URL. To scan a QR code, open the camera on your phone as if you were going to take a picture. Without pressing anything, point the camera at the QR code. As long as the QR code is large enough and the camera is in focus, the camera will automatically scan the code and a QR icon will light up near the bottom of the screen. When you tap the icon, it will reveal a link. Press the link, and you will head to the webpage. If your camera does not read QR code well, you can also download one of many free QR code reader apps.

- I have looked at my phone in the last 10 minutes.
- I get pop-up notifications from more than six apps.
- Today I have sought information on my phone (answer to a question, directions, etc.).
- I check my phone without intention or prompting.
- I rely on my phone for time and task management (alarms, reminders, calendars).
- I have used my phone's digital wellbeing/screen time feature to check how often my screen is unlocked and in what apps.
- I have social media apps on my home screen.
- I use social media to learn from others in my profession or field of interest.
- I have watched a video on my phone in the last 24 hours.
- I look at content on my phone while I am _____
  - waiting in a long line.
  - waiting for a meeting or event to begin.
  - eating.
  - commuting/traveling.
  - winding down for the day.
  - generally bored.
  - Other: _____
- I have checked my phone's record of screen active time.
- I play podcasts from my phone.
- I read _____ on my phone.
  - emails
  - articles
  - books
  - Other: _____
- I take notes on my phone.
- I take photos of learning materials I want to save and consult at a later time (e.g., book pages, presentation slides).
  - I typically consult and apply these materials at a later time.
- I use apps on my phone specifically for learning (e.g., flashcards, languages, courses).
- If I see an article on my phone that I want to read later, I have a useful process for saving that article.

This checklist is a simple way to begin reflecting on your mobile phone habits: Are you on your phone often? How much use is intentional versus ambient? Where and how do you learn and work? Overall, is your phone usage what you want it to be, or would you like to make changes? What mobile tech practices would you like to decrease, and which would you like to increase?

Oddly enough, my interest in mobile-mindful learning started with skepticism about phones. Technology-based distraction is often a barrier to the deep attention needed for creativity and production. We have likely heard about emails, notifications, and social media as productivity foes. In those many short, spare moments with nothing to do, I found myself mindlessly scrolling through Facebook when I didn't really like Facebook in the first place. I resolved to reduce and rewire my mobile tech habits: Along with recommendations from the Center for Humane Technology (2021) on how to take control of our phone habits and interactions, I began to pause before unlocking my screen to consider if this was the time to leave my phone alone or to access something that would benefit my learning and relationships. It is with this intention that I became a mobile-mindful learner.

Choosing to access your phone less is a great option when you are with family and friends, enjoying an experience, or attending to an important matter. When your environment is not providing meaningful interaction, having intentional, diverse mobile learning opportunities can help you read more books, keep up on timely articles, and maintain meaningful networks and relationships. Creating a more fluid, intentional design for continuity can increase productivity and creativity. When I resolved to rewire my phone behavior habits toward mobile learning, I thought about what I wished I had more time to learn. For example, I wanted to expand my breadth of knowledge on pedagogy and read more books. As an educational developer, my work is improved by being a generalist more than a specialist, keeping up with teaching trends, theories, strategies, and stories. At the moment, my "books to read" list is 45 titles deep, and I'm sure many are missing.

From here, I channeled my novice mobile-mindful powers to create fluid learning opportunities surrounding these goals. I resolved to read books on my phone, which was a dreaded mobile learning moment at first. I was late to the podcast game but dove in right away to many podcasts related to teaching in higher education. As a result, my learning multiplied exponentially. I not only learned content, but I learned through conversation, voices, and personalities. Learning is social, after all.

I love print books, and reading on a phone screen felt like a betrayal of my literary values. Nevertheless, I found that reading on a phone increased my reading capacity and offered new ways of being an active reader. I'm the type of reader who does not mind reading a few books simultaneously, so I achieved a different type of fluid learning by having books of different modes available at any point in time. The Mobile Reading section in chapter 3 explores increasing mobile reading options in strategic ways conducive to phones and how phones can help us add a digital component to our print reading.

TIP: CHECK YOUR PHONE LESS WITH A SMARTWATCH

During the part of my productivity workshop on reducing phone distractions, a participant lamented that she couldn't easily tuck away her phone because her son had health concerns that required her to be reached for emergencies. This resulted in constantly checking her phone, which resulted in her engaging in more mobile-mindless app-opening and scrolling. A fellow participant recommended using a smartwatch, which helped her know when something needed her attention but allowed her distance from her phone screen otherwise. With a smartwatch it is important to limit notifications so that your wrist is not constantly buzzing, but once those notifications are reined in, it can help reduce our phone-checking muscle memory.

Your Mobile Learning Portrait: Material and Environmental Learning Conditions

Before getting into all of the apps, strategies, and resources you can use to do more mobile learning, we have to first describe who we are currently as mobile learners. We have to acknowledge where and how we learn, the intentional and unintentional mobility within that learning, and reflect on what has and has not worked for us. More importantly, we will recognize how learning is happening all of the time without our notice. When I started paying attention to the material and environmental conditions of my academic work and learning, I saw my work less as isolated sessions and more as focused work sessions connected by countless thoughts and experiences. Only by seeing the larger current of our learning lives can we include more mobile-mindful strategies.

Mapping our learning is particularly important because we may be tempted to see academic work as either place-bound or placeless rather than as place-conscious. Our academic work may also seem very sedentary, perhaps in front of a screen or a book. When we really pay attention, though, we see that we are making choices about where and how we work all the time, and that we may have more choices than we have taken advantage of. In *The*

Extended Mind, Annie Murphy Paul (2021) explored the ways that thinking happens beyond our minds, even beyond our bodies. She covered four aspects of the extended mind: thinking through our bodies, our environments, other people, and through devices. We might expect to stick with the devices aspect for mobile-mindful learning, but all of these types of thinking come into play with mobile-mindful learning.

We became painfully aware of our environmental links to knowledge work when many of us had to work from home during the COVID-19 pandemic. There were some clear advantages to working from home for those who had the luxury of doing so: no commute, fewer distractions, fewer expenses related to eating out, and the overall comfort some enjoyed at home. There were also clear disadvantages, especially as working from home was under duress of a serious illness and meant that many parents were also caring for and supervising the schooling of their children.

Less expected outcomes emerged as well: We saw the effects of being unmoored from our motion-, time-, and environment-based routines. The "fake commute" is perhaps the best example: Once people recognized that their commute was a valuable mental process ritual, some implemented a process of leaving the house, taking a ride or drive to simulate what one would do to get to the office, and going through other commute-related routines to begin and end the workday (Cassata, 2020; Rogers, 2021). People started paying attention to what the commute yielded: Psychologist Jamie Goldstein described the commute as an example of segmentation, or crucial transitions that helped people conclude one part of their day and prepare for the next part of their day (Cassata, 2020). Travel time provided "reflection time and thinking time" (Rogers, 2021, para. 6), the type of thinking our bodies enable away from a computer. We can go further to explore the cognitive benefits of walking—particularly in nature—a habit many great thinkers considered crucial to their work (Pang, 2016; Paul, 2021). At times, we may find a change of scene energizes our thinking work and helps us see things from a different perspective. Additionally, indigenous communities have long recognized learning as an environmental and social place-based way of being (e.g., Johnson, 2012; American Indian College Fund, 2018).

As I prompt often throughout this book, let's start by taking notice of our current working and thinking actions:

1. Where do you work? Do you have one workplace, or multiple?
2. What type of atmosphere most inspires your thinking as it concerns people, places, motion, materials, and other elements?

3. On what electronic and tactile devices do you work? When do you use each medium, and why? Is one better for certain types of tasks, phases of work, and sequences of tasks?
4. How do you keep your different workplaces, devices, and materials connected? Does one type of work feed into another?
5. Where do you encounter barriers? In what situations do you find it difficult to think clearly or develop ideas? What do you find hard to keep track of?

In reflecting on these questions and using them to observe your own behaviors, you may notice that while you might favor specific work modes, you are working in more mobile ways than you might have expected. You might label "work" that perhaps doesn't look or feel like work, such as an aha! moment during a conversation with a colleague. You might notice that you are on a laptop more than a desktop, which makes you more inclined to "work from wherever" rather than in an office (if you have one). You might admit that while writing in a notepad feels inefficient, it gives a boost to your work so that you have more to type when you are in front of the computer.

I hope you also notice barriers, such as the fact that little from the notebook actually makes it into the digital formats that ultimately form your written publications. You might notice that while you hear useful things in podcasts, you lack a good process for connecting them to your teaching work. You might find it useful to plot out plans on your office whiteboard but often find yourself in another space wondering what you had written back on that whiteboard. You might find that while your desktop computer has a large screen, you avoid working on it because it takes a long time to start up. You might get a judgy notification from your phone's photo app asking if you would like to delete the 12 photos you took of print book pages. You might generally notice you are more sedentary than you would like to be but can't imagine doing any productive work in motion.

This is a great point for identifying barriers associated with our material and environmental work conditions, even if those problems seem vague and unsolvable. Such work unseats assumptions many of us hold about learning and other academic work: that if we sit still enough, know enough, have the best tools and the fewest distractions, our brain should produce good work. This type of mindset sees our environment almost as an adversary to thinking when, in reality, our environment should not only be conducive to thinking but also be a conduit for thinking.

After acknowledging where and how you currently learn, let's consider how to increase learning with mobile devices. We will explore options for learning via reading and multimodal formats, learning with others, and organizing it all across time, space, and devices.

References

American Indian College Fund. (2018, June 4). *Place-based learning as a framework for building native student success.* IECE. https://collegefund.org/blog/place-based-learning-framework-building-native-student-success/

Cassata, C. (2020, November 12). Why adding a "fake commute" to your wfh schedule could help you unwind. *Healthline.* https://www.healthline.com/health-news/why-adding-a-fake-commute-to-your-wfh-schedule-could-help-you-unwind

Center for Humane Technology. (2021). *Take control.* humanetech.com/take-control

Hokanson, B. (2014). Rich and remote learning and cognition: Analog methods as models for newer technology. In C. Miller & A. Doering (Eds.), *The new landscape of mobile learning* (pp. 42–55). Routledge.

Johnson, J. T. (2012). Place-based learning and knowing: Critical pedagogies grounded in Indigeneity. *GeoJournal, 75*(1). https://doi.org/10.1007/s10708-010-9379-1

Pang, A. S. (2016). *Rest: Why you get more done when you work less.* Basic Books.

Paul, A. M. (2021). *The extended mind: The power of thinking outside the brain.* Mariner Books.

Rogers, K. (2021, January 18). The rise of the fake commute, and why it's good for your mental health. *CNN.* https://www.cnn.com/2021/01/18/success/fake-commute-meaning-benefits-pandemic-wellness/index.html

Selfe, C. L. (1999). Technology and literacy: A story about the perils of not paying attention. *College Composition and Communication, 50*(3), 411–436. https://doi.org/10.2307/358859

Stachowiak, B. (Host). (2019, January 17). Small teaching online (No. 240) [Audio podcast episode]. In *Teaching in higher ed.* https://teachinginhighered.com/podcast/small-teaching-online

Tobin, T., & Behling, K. T. (2018). Meet the mobile learners. *Reach everyone, teach everyone: Universal design for learning in higher education.* Western Virginia University Press.

3

MOBILE LEARNING BASIC
SKILLS AND CONTENT

While most of us have logged countless hours on our phones, there may be some basic features and skills we have not practiced. These basics can build up your mobile-mindful learning strategies. Check off the ones you have done, and make a plan for trying the ones that you have not. While these features are available on just about every smartphone, the exact process might vary by operating system and device. Therefore, do an internet search for how to do the skills you are not familiar with, including your phone model.

- Identify a few main learning tools that work well on a computer and smartphone. They should be tools you like using and that serve multiple purposes. Tools could include programs used for taking notes, storing information, and communicating with groups.
- Identify one or two preferred apps for audio and video content. Within these apps, explore content that fits your mobile learning goals (e.g., podcasts, YouTube channels, and the people and organizations who produce such content) and use their curation mechanisms such as subscription and playlists. See the Recommended Apps: Multimedia Platforms section at the end of the book for potential apps you could use.
- Move app icons to different screens on your phone, usually by holding down the icon and dragging it to the desired location. This move brings to the forefront apps you want to access in your free time and pushes away apps you want to engage with less. If you use many apps, you can also bundle them into folders by category or function.

- Cull your notifications by holding down a push notification and selecting your desired notification frequency or by going into an individual app's settings to change how you receive notifications. Also check out the Notifications section of your phone settings to customize default notification parameters such as sound, visibility, and timing.
- Use voice-to-text to type an email, text message, or note. (Usually a microphone button is available on the phone's keyboard.) Voice-to-text will type out words as you speak aloud, including some simple punctuation.
- Check how long you have been on your phone today. (Phones more commonly have a built-in feature that tracks when the screen is activated. Check your phone's Settings area.)
- Copy-paste useful text from something you are reading on your phone and transfer it to an appropriate note-taking location.
- Use the "Share" feature to post content (e.g., photos, articles) on social media or curate in another location. The universal "Share" icon is one dot with two lines branching out to two dots (see Figure 3.1). When you click on this icon, you will be presented with multiple options for where to send or share the content, such as storage spaces (Google Drive, Dropbox), email, social media, and tasks.
- Take a screenshot, which is turning what you currently see on your phone screen into a photo file. Actions for taking a screenshot can differ based on the phone, so do an internet search if you are not sure. Use the "Share" feature to save it somewhere you can use later.
- Install a web extension version of a phone app. Web extensions allow you to connect any webpage you visit with an app, such as apps for annotation, collecting articles, and creating tasks. For example, with an Instapaper web extension, you can click on one button to automatically save the webpage you are reading to the Instapaper App. Extensions can also add features to your browser of choice, such as recording the screen with one click. While this skill focuses on a computer, it allows for a more fluid connection to content you might later access on your phone.

Figure 3.1. "Share" icon.

Figure 3.2. Web extension for Todoist task organizer program.

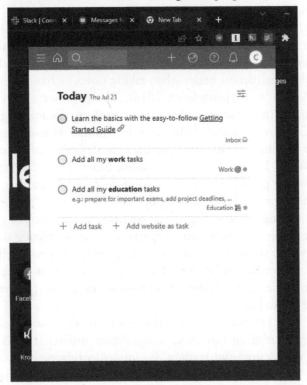

The web browser extension for Todoist, a productivity app that manages tasks, allows you to add your current website to a task. As shown at the top of Figure 3.2, the toolbar pins multiple extensions (Instapaper, Hypothesis, Todoist) while all others appear in a dropdown list when pressing the puzzle piece button in Chrome.

Once you have these basics in place, you will be ready to engage in different forms of mobile learning.

Mobile Reading

While we learn through many different modes and actions, reading written text is likely the most common mode of learning new concepts in higher education, from weighty textbooks and journal articles to narrative books and reports. We may accept digital reading as a valid medium for reading PDF articles and shorter pieces on computers, but our skepticism may spike when we imagine students reading course content on their phones. Instead, let's pause to identify possibilities in getting the most out of every reading mode available to students.

A few research studies have been cited frequently to condemn digital devices for learning and even promote technology bans, such as the popular "pen is mightier than the keyboard" study suggesting that students comprehend class instruction better when taking notes by hand rather than by laptop (Mueller & Oppenheimer, 2014). The presence of any data may sway us toward our bias toward the print medium for learning, although these studies largely acknowledge that intentional note-taking strategies are a more significant learning factor than the devices used for note-taking (Miller, 2022). Jenae Cohn's (2021) book *Skim, Dive, Surface: Teaching Digital Reading* provided a critical reading of research that has been used to close the door on digital reading options, saying that "an inertia gap is at play in reading at the college level: we keep trying to apply print-based reading strategies to digital reading spaces, but upon realizing those strategies don't work, we move toward blaming the digital space itself" (p. 13). The same argument can be made for mobile learning, as our print-based learning strategies certainly don't lend themselves to smartphones, and the phones are left to blame.

Cohn (2021) instead argued that more practice and skill-building around digital reading can make a significant difference, and the same applies to mobile-mindful reading. By implementing new processes, routines, and tools for digital reading, we may find digital reading to be an acceptable alternative to print reading and even superior in certain cases. Importantly, Cohn provided guidance on how to teach these digital reading skills to students so that when they do read on a laptop or mobile device, they are getting the most out of their reading. In talking with her students, she found the following:

> Many of them did their readings on their phones during the bus ride to campus or on their laptops in between classes, perched in a hallway or at the campus cafeteria. We all had lots of choices for how, when, and where to read, but we weren't talking explicitly about how to navigate these choices. (p. 4)

Cohn is a proponent of offering effective fluid learning experiences rather than sealing off learning from digital devices.

As we "start with self" in exploring mobile-mindful learning, identify your current digital reading habits (or lack thereof):

1. Do you feel a strong preference for reading digitally or in print? What is behind the preference? Does this preference change based on the reading occasion?

2. What do you read on your phone, and why? What is the greatest length piece you tend to read? How much do you read on a phone for learning versus entertainment?
3. What barriers do you experience in your reading modes? Does writing notes on journal article printouts mean you have to spend extra time transcribing those annotations in a digital format? Do you find digital annotations difficult?

Questions like these can help you describe what is automatic or unnoticed about your reading actions and explore new possibilities. Let's explore some of those possibilities.

Reading Books on a Phone: A Fluid Learning Example

I never understood how my husband could read a 32-book sci-fi series entirely on his phone, but that's how he does all of his leisure reading. I explored my feelings around reading in print, such as knowing at a glance where I am in the trajectory of the book and noticing how quickly I turn the pages when I am engrossed. Eventually, I admitted I was not doing as much leisure reading as I wanted, both for entertainment and learning. I suspected that adding some mobile reading options would boost my reading capacity, which proved to be true. Reading some books on my phone allowed me to participate in book clubs I otherwise would not have and read nonfiction I would otherwise likely not get to.

Then, as a graduate student in educational leadership, I considered reading one of my required texts on my phone. Its narrative structure made it conducive to reading in a granular format, that is, in small chunks. I was willing to use Kindle's annotation tools to take notes I might need for class discussion or writing. We read the book a chapter at a time and were required to only read about half of the book chapters. The book's purpose for our class was to flesh out our overall understanding of historical events leading up to our research projects. Class activities and projects would not require frequent citation and textual analysis. While the convenience of having one of my required texts on my phone was the main factor, the Kindle version was $6 as opposed to $26 in print. Before buying the Kindle version, I asked the professor if she had objections to me reading in this format, such as my potential ability to refer to page numbers, but she trusted my judgment on picking a reading format. (Clearly I recalled my English major days when professors insisted on everyone reading the same edition of a book so we had the same page numbers.)

Reading this book on my phone worked out well: While there were other course books I bought in print, this book was my go-to digital read, which was particularly important during summer 2020 when the

COVID-19 pandemic meant I was managing work without childcare for two young children. I found myself able to take fuller notes because could use voice-to-text to talk through responses to parts of the text via the Kindle app instead of the few words I would have been able to scribble in a half-inch page margin. In the interest of fluid learning, I also explored Kindle's Cloud Reader and how to export annotations. The Cloud Reader is the computer version of reading the digital book, which allows the option to see page numbers as they appear in print, which worked fine for the class since it was online anyway. Plus, I could export the annotations so that I could save them in a document to consult when it was time to write discussion forum posts or papers.

In this example, fluid reading was not making every course text available on print, computer, and phone but making some of the course reading available in any of those modes. I had a designated text for mobile reading, two books in print, and smaller articles for the computer (which could also be printed). By finding where this balance could work with our own reading, we may then be able to facilitate fluid learning opportunities for students as well. As in this case, planning these opportunities may be as simple as being aware of which course texts have e-book options and guiding students' choices in whether to read e-versions or print versions. Not all students will go through the consideration I went through on how well I would read and take notes in an e-version, so walking through a few recommendations could go a long way. In the chapter 9 case studies, I applied similar analysis and recommendations to a travel literature class.

Digitizing Print Reading and Note-Taking

As much I love the efficiency and capability of digital modes, I still cherish writing and reading on paper. Sometimes in the writing process it helps me to slow down and parse out what is most important in my work. It makes work *feel* and *look* in ways I find motivating after too many hours looking at Arial font atop glowing white pages. In *Extending the Mind*, Paul (2021) explained that the brain needs to be able to situate ideas visually, which can be difficult with a single screen or monitor, much less a very small screen.

I could claim that books and other print media are the original mobile tech in comparison to the libraries holding scrolls of antiquity, but my discussion of print modes is more in the interest of fluid learning and how mobile learning can actually make the most of our print-based work. The mobile-mindful learning challenge here is to use your phone to capture your offline learning in a way that can then be used online. Pairing mobile note-taking with print reading has been a huge fluid learning win for me. When I want to capture a quote or develop a reflection while reading a print book, I most often use voice-to-text within a document or note-taking app. This is quicker and less distracting than typing on my phone or laptop or writing by hand, and I don't have to type out fuller notes later. Google Lens offers more robust ways to digitize print reading, from copying text to translation, web searches, and decoding.

APP HIGHLIGHT: GOOGLE LENS TRANSCRIBES THE OFFLINE WORLD

The Google Lens app uses augmented reality (AR) to do a variety of processes through your camera. If you are reading a print book and want to capture a paragraph to quote or write about later, you can point your camera at the page, use the Select Text option, and the app will be able to read the text and give you options on whether to copy-paste or directly share to another place. This feature has saved me from the time-consuming process of typing a paragraph while awkwardly holding open a print book.

If you decide to write by hand, the Google Lens app may be able to transcribe your handwriting into digital form. I practiced on a short weekly reflection I wrote by hand. While my handwriting is fairly neat, it had underlining and bullets that I thought would throw off the transcription. The result was almost perfect. The bullet format did not translate well, but all of the words were there.

In addition to digitizing print text from your camera, the app can translate languages and perform photo-based searches to provide location-based information, identify plants, and more. When I was reading the sci-fi novel *The City We Became* by N.K. Jemisin, its cover art became animated art when viewed through Google Lens. Use the QR code (Figure 3.3) to explore the app for many potential uses for your mobile learning and as an option for your students. I predominantly use it to copy-paste text when I am reading a print book or to digitally transcribe my handwritten notes.

Figure 3.3. lens.google shows the many uses and applications for the Google Lens app.

Recommendations for Mobile-Mindful Reading

- Reflect on how you currently read offline and online, identifying affordances and struggles.
- Dabble in reading e-books for learning purposes.
- Explore annotation capabilities within mobile e-readers and how they translate to a computer.
- Include mobile reading as a part of a larger reading landscape, choosing which reading works well on a phone and what may work better in print or on a computer.
- When reading print materials, explore ways to digitize the active reading process by using voice-to-text to capture quotes and notes or capturing passages and handwritten notes in photos or other digital transcription.

Audio Learning With Podcasts, Interviews, Books, and Courses

I was an early audio learner, although not at all mobile. I sat in front of my home's cassette player to follow along with Hooked on Phonics lessons. I still remember the cream-colored tapes in a huge book-like plastic container, and the cadence of sounding out each letter along with how they sounded in select words. After going through intensive speech therapy, these exercises gave me an extra boost of language fluency. Audio learning has come a long way since then, or audio consumption at least. Podcasts help us pass the time. Audio books help us get through more books than we ever could by visual reading alone. Audio content provides the opportunity to hear authentic voices rather than only the voice we produce in our heads while reading. Through interviews, students experience the authors of their course texts as real people.

When I talk with instructors about mobile learning, they often speak of offering lectures and readings in an audio format. International studies instructor Carol Hart assigned six travel narratives for her travel literature course and was surprised to find that students took advantage of audio forms when they were available. She had not considered this option until her students told her they listened to texts during the commute to campus (personal communication, May 12, 2022). Nursing instructor Lynda Poly-Droulard has also recognized, "The class commute is often the best time for students to focus on the courses without interruption" (personal communication, March 30, 2022). She credits audio options with the main way her Fundamentals of Nursing Practice students can get through her narrated slides in her flipped classroom model. In UDL and fluid learning fashion, Poly-Droulard offers her lectures as narrated PowerPoints in three files on the LMS: slides only, narrated slides, and audio-only. Her students can flip through the slides when they are on a computer or phone, and then reinforce the content with her audio explanations as they travel to class. Producing the audio-only option requires exporting an mp3 from the narrated PowerPoint she has already created. Her course text also offers a read-aloud format, so students can rely on an audio format for most of the instructional content. A deeper dive into Hart's and Poly-Droulard's mobile-mindful teaching practices and opportunities are offered in the case studies in chapter 9.

Audio learning options can open access to learning, both by direct access to information at more places and times and for more ways to engage with the material. Students show a strong use of and preference for audio learning formats (Smydra, 2022). In a study of 434 students, 64% said they accessed and listened to assigned podcasts on a regular basis (Gachago et al., 2016). Like many of us, students might be more inclined to listen to a 50-minute podcast episode than read an article for 20 minutes since they can listen on their commute. Award-winning educator Michael Wesch (2019) encouraged reading to students to the point of making every single class reading and video text available on an audio playlist. In doing so, some of his students claimed they were doing the reading for the first time ever. Additionally, he had a conversation with students as he read, which simultaneously taught students that reading should be a conversation that engages their reflections and past experiences.

In talking about audio learning on the ThinkUDL podcast with host Lillian Nave (2020), she shared that she seeks opportunities to bring audio into the classroom when teaching intercultural dialogues so that students can hear people of different cultures tell their own stories in their own voices. The curriculum is not just the words, but the way in which those words are expressed. While audio can provide an alternative format for learning material, the same learning will not take place as visually reading a text or experiencing knowledge in another form. Therefore, consider not only what is available in audio form, but what type of learning is made available in any given audio content.

As educators, we should distinguish between audio consumption and true audio learning. While we might listen to informational content, are we actually learning from it? How do we know? To use educator Terry Doyle's popular saying, "The one who does the work does the learning" (Honeycutt, 2022). The axiom goes for learning in any medium, but podcasts' prevalence is due to our ability to multitask while listening since our eyes and hands are not required in the process. Instead of discounting audio learning due to potential distraction or passive consumption, let's instead consider how to do the work of learning as we listen.

Arresting Bias Against Audio Reading

The assumption that visual reading is better for learning than listening can have consequences for our students and, in turn, the learning environments we create. I am a sighted person who has learning preferences that fit into education's norms: As an English major I loved reading print books, preferably scribbling notes into the margins, underlining important lines, and then organizing main points into a lined notebook. This process matched most of my professors' ways of knowing, which likely helped me produce papers they recognized as scholarly, which likely helped my success as a graduate student and researcher.

An overemphasis on visual texts, including visual reading, risks unnecessarily excluding those who are blind and dyslexic, those whose cultures emphasize oral traditions, or more simply those with a strong preference and skill for spoken expression. Rather than determining which mode of reading and learning is superior, consider how to best present choices and variety, which increases opportunities for all learners. Then, dig into the real questions of learning: What actions are involved in "good reading"? What does good reading enable? Such questions help us recognize different types of reading and their usefulness to the course learning goals.

For example, we might be proponents of "active reading," meaning students are not passively letting words wash over them but are taking notes, identifying key ideas, and responding to the ideas presented. Passive reading is a challenge whether one is dragging their eyeballs across written lines on a page or listening to voices buzzing in the background. Just as we should design visual reading with active components, we should do the same with audio reading. We can start with prompting learners to take a "podcast pause" during and at the end of an assigned episode, or whenever students recognize a key point in an audio book.

The Podcast Pause

Many scholars of teaching argue for the importance of summarizing and reflecting on a learning experience as that experience concludes, which helps our brain process, situate, and store this information and determine its relevance. When we switch swiftly from one task to the next, our brain fails to encode the learning experience effectively. As I became more mobile-mindful in my audio learning, I challenged myself to hit the pause button more frequently while listening to podcasts or books. What I would do during that pause differed based on my learning goals: If I was listening to ideas that I would likely write about later, I paused to capture ideas I would want to write about or create a task to look through the transcript to quote a particular idea. If my goals focused on personal reflection, I paused to simply let the idea sink in and to give my mind space to focus on why a particular point seemed important, usually articulating the connection to my past. I sometimes even talked through these reflections. No matter my learning goals, I paused at the end of every episode before letting the next episode in the queue play to articulate what ideas were most relevant to me and what actions I wanted to take accordingly.

These pauses are powerful. At a sensory level, the pauses are clearer than pauses we might take while reading a written text: While the written text still remains in front of us, pausing audio transitions us to silence immediately. My podcast listening is a blend of entertainment and learning, and like any other reading experience I am not always sure how much I will learn from an episode. Now I am in more of a pausing routine: When I realize that a podcast episode I am listening to relates closely to something I have experienced or am working on, I remember that I should pause and articulate that "something."

While pauses are a great start, we could take more intentional actions during those pauses, especially if we are designing the audio learning content. If we scale up to audio lessons, audio courses such as those designed by Alpe Audio and Listenable provide a useful example of audio designed for intentional learning.

Audio Courses

Podcasts are likely the most popular way to consume audio content. We tend to listen and remember some content, but mostly leave it up to our brains to keep what it will and forget the rest. Audio courses, however, have a more intentional design with learning objectives, pauses for review, and opportunities to recall important concepts. Such courses will also have connected lessons contributing to learning goals. The Alpe app is an example of this type of audio learning, with a range of audio courses. Alpe Audio has designed courses with careful attention to lesson length, pacing, chunking, curriculum concepts, audio cues, review, and recall opportunities (Zlotogorski, 2020). This approach provides a good comparison point of what type of learning we can expect podcast episodes to provide versus intentional curriculum built for audio (Honeycutt, n.d.). Taking an audio course will help you experience the difference of intentional learning design in audio versus listening to the latest episode of a podcast.

Like Alpe Audio, Listenable produces its own audio courses at a subscription cost, made up of around 10 lessons, each 5 minutes long. (Alpe and Listenable are listed among other Mobile Learning Tools in Appendix B.) While Listenable's courses are on a range of everyday practice topics, Learn Out Loud curates hundreds of free courses produced by universities, linking out to iTunes files, YouTube videos, and LibriVox, among many others. LibriVox is a database of public domain books read and produced in audio-book format by volunteers. Browsing free databases like Learn Out Loud and LibriVox could help inform course text choices, especially in courses that are more likely to draw on materials in the public domain. From these websites, you can download audio files (often mp3 format) that can be saved some-where you can access on a phone.

Visual Learning With Videos, Photos, and Slide Decks

Like podcasts, we may watch videos here and there, but without an inten-tional learning practice attached to our viewing. Similar to audio learning, I encourage paying attention to how visual learning such as watching videos, browsing photo collections, and going through slide decks can fit into mobile learning specifically and fluid learning generally. As with other elements of the Start with Self mobile-mindful learning approach, first take notice of your current visual media consumption on smartphones and other modali-ties, especially those that contribute to your learning. Then, reflect on how these actions can be harnessed into intentional, applicable learning practices.

Visual learning as used here refers to learning from visual media beyond alphabetic text. Some media may include more alphabetic text than others, but include more visual formats such as:

- videos
- infographics
- photo albums, such as those in archives
- slide decks, which may also include audio narrated elements
- maps
- games

Take notice of how you currently learn through these modes and how to best capture and apply what you learn through them. See the Recommended Apps in Appendix B for visual media apps to try.

When Do Photos Help or Hinder Learning?

When a key data point strikes us at a presentation, we might quickly snap a photo of the projected slide. While reading a book, we might take pictures of key passages. If you have done this, how often do you remember the con-tent in those photos or do something with those photos? It is not promising when your phone's photo app asks if you're ready to archive those 10 pictures of book pages. In *Remembering and Forgetting in the Age of Technology*, Miller (2022) specifically addressed this question of whether taking a picture actually makes it last longer, and provided a nuanced answer: Intention and follow-up action matter (p. 186). If we take a photo to postpone actively engaging the content we are capturing (i.e., disengaging at that moment), we will remember it less than if we hadn't taken the photo at all, as Miller shared from a study of photo-taking during a field trip (Tamir et al., 2018). But if we do something with the photo, such as create a task on what to do with that idea or jot down a mobile note of what resonated with us about the slide, we are more likely to remember and apply it.

Next time you reach for your phone to take a picture of something for a learning purpose, ask yourself why this is worth taking a photo and either do something with it right at that moment or implement a process for regularly returning to these photos. The Curating Your Learning section in chapter 4 provides strategies for processing mobile content.

A Case in Mobile Learning: Video Playlist Related to Research Study

As an ethnographic study, my dissertation research required collecting a variety of cultural artifacts (Moore, 2021). I conducted a digital ethnography of "#ungrading" as a teaching-based online community of practice. I would study some online spaces more closely and regularly, and others would be minor but still provide the variety needed to get the whole picture of the learning and community culture. I focused most of my attention on Twitter, book club activities, and blogs, but to get a fuller picture of how these ideas spread through other media and people, I also explored ungrading-based presentations shared on YouTube. To get the most out of reviewing these presentations without spending too much time in this minor area, I had to employ strategic mobile learning moves.

I curated a playlist of ungrading presentation videos so that I could easily pull them up while doing simple, everyday tasks that required little attention. Listening to them at a quicker speed allowed me to get the idea of the message. Since I was listening for presenters' references to social learning development around ungrading rather than to learn about ungrading itself, I did not have to actively engage with content the whole time. When I thought something was important to note, I would pause the video, access a Google Doc on video presentations, and take notes via voice-to-text. Then I would resume playing through the video.

This example shows how mobile learning can both bolster more focused learning on a computer and be a useful mode on its own. This type of video research was better conducted on a mobile device than on a laptop, although it could have been done on a laptop as well. Seeing learning tasks in this way is crucial for aligning the time you have with what you want to accomplish without adding an unreasonable amount of work.

Recommendations for Audio and Visual Learning

- *Identify what type of multimodal content meets your mobile learning goals.* Curate playlists on whatever app may best work for you, such as platforms specific to podcasts (PodBean, Google Podcasts, Apple Podcasts) and broader audio content (Spotify, Apple Music), video (YouTube, Vimeo), or a broader range of visual media (photo albums, slide decks, even highly visual social media like Instagram and TikTok).
- *Evaluate whether the multimodal content includes helpful text alternatives and accompaniments,* such as captions, transcripts, and resource lists. Notice both the real and potential usefulness of these components in your learning.
- *Identify a multimodal component that boosts your mobile learning goals in more than one way.* Does it show the people and places related to the content? Were you able to read a book more quickly by audio? Is it read by the author?
- *Reflect on your learning process as you listen or watch.* Do you remember what you listened to and saw? How did you apply the learning: Did you take notes, capture a quote, save the link to include somewhere else, and refer to the material in conversation or somewhere else? What did you experience through multimedia that you might not have otherwise experienced by alphabetic reading alone?
- *Practice "the Pause."* Whenever part of a podcast, book, or video seems particularly important or makes you think of something, pause to capture and develop that response. The pause helps you not only process the content but also prevents you from ignoring the content while you are processing that thought.
- *Listen to an audio course.* How is the learning experience different from other types of audio content?
- *Stretch what it means to learn by audio and visual media*: Are there stories, songs, photography, poetry, sound effects, and other multimodal content that contribute to learning about a topic?
- *Create your own multimodal content as a part of your learning process.* What are you able to express or process that is different from typing or writing? Expressions could include audio recording, visual note-taking, infographics, and memes.

Social Learning With Social Media and Group Platforms

We take for granted how social learning is. On the one hand, social learning and social practice theory understand knowledge and reality as being built collectively through our norms, exchanges, diversity, and connections. On the other hand, formal school environments tend to be fixed on individualism. While we praise collaboration and community and try to include more group work, educational norms are focused on individuals hunched over books, writing papers, taking tests, and getting good grades. Mobile learning tends to take this same individualistic approach. Upon evaluating iPad use for educational purposes, educators found that mobile apps were strongly catered to individual consumption and testing rather than collaboration and creation, which impeded more mobile tech integration into schools (Murray & Olcese, 2011).

Social media use has increased exponentially since this 2011 study, but only the tech-adventurous were considering how to include social media into courses. Social media provides great learning options, with a range of public and private options. Facebook Groups provide a semiprivate space to have easy access to people of similar experience, identity, or purpose. LinkedIn provides a professionalism that many perceive as escaping the vitriol and superfluousness of other social media. Twitter provides vast opportunities to learn from others by following scholars, authors, colleagues, and important voices underrecognized in your field of interest. TikTok helps teachers reach the public in engaging, super-short videos. While Twitter and TikTok can be browsed without an account, social learning also includes your social involvement.

Learning ecologies and fluid learning take social learning into account. The nonformal category of learning ecologies usually consists of communities and networks: The ecology is not just made up of the place or platform but the people who occupy them. Likewise, one of fluid learning's five characteristics is interactivity, which can include the response we get from other people. Perhaps even more fitting is the "ubiquity" characteristic: Social media helps faculty and students see how learning opportunities are everywhere and can happen anywhere, from retweeting and adding a course hashtag to video-responses to TikTok posts.

Social media might be another *ugh* in our feeling about mobile tech. The drama. The outrage. The selfies. The trolling. The chasing of likes and retweets. The "me me me" of it (Stein, 2013). Social media platforms are among the highest offenders of spurring addictive behaviors and sucking the productivity out of our days. While there are plenty of reasons to be wary of our social media diet, some psychologists and tech researchers tease out what makes social media good and bad. Anticipating we would set our new year's resolutions on nixing social media from our lives, *Psychology Today* published "Don't Resolve to Use Social Media Less. Resolve to Use It Better" on January 1, 2020. In the article Sarah Rose Cavanagh, psychologist and author of *The Spark of Learning* and *Hivemind,* took an expert dive into how we can increase the quality of our social media activity by ensuring we use these platforms to "enhance" rather than "eclipse" our existing relationships and cultivate meaningful new relationships. Cavanagh goes into much more depth on this topic in her book *Hivemind,* which describes how the collective and social nature of humans explain the challenges and triumphs of tribalism. In short, we should consider the benefits of learning from others on social media and mitigate the less constructive features.

I had never been particularly drawn to social media. I took a stab at Twitter and LinkedIn many years ago but didn't find the spaces worth the attention. But knowing that part of mobile-mindful learning is social learning, I revisited my purpose and strategy in these spaces. On Twitter I culled who I was following, following only accounts who represented specific humans such as people I had listened to on podcasts, authors I had read, and people I had met at conferences. Eventually, I also followed those who popped up in the same conversations I did and consistently shared ideas I appreciated. I did the same on LinkedIn. Within months of reengaging in these spaces as a listener and participant, I learned so much from people and made meaningful connections with many of them.

Mobile learning with social media is also not as all-or-nothing as it seems. Most people exist somewhere between the no-profile-picture person with three followers and the superstar who is balancing being adored and loathed by the masses. Two good places to start might be developing a profile that shares what you want to be publicly known about you and then sharing, resharing, and commenting on other people's content. This active listening and engagement is highly appreciated and a way to break the ice with people in your field or simply people who interest you.

If you determine social media should have no place in your mobile-mindful learning, consider what other forms mobile-mindful social learning could take. If you are part of a book club, an on-and-off-again writing group, or a loose network of people with a similar interest, consider organizing them in a more private online group that makes for easy communication and information sharing through tools like Slack or Discord. For a larger group, seek out platforms made for communities of practice such as Mighty Networks, which are similar to Facebook Groups in their closed community capability but offer more robust engagement options such as calendars, events, subgroups, and topic threads. These types of tools and groups pull social media's good features into a private, more focused group. Since the

COVID-19 pandemic, instructors have been using such private group platforms for teaching development groups (Moore, 2021) and class communication (e.g., "Slack Enhances Communication for Students," 2022). These and more apps are listed in the Social Learning and Community Building section of Appendix B.

TIP: MAKING SOCIAL MEDIA CONTENT ACCESSIBLE

Social media is crucial for receiving timely information, discovering new voices and stories, and for our entertainment. Unfortunately, people with visual and other disabilities encounter many barriers to fully engaging in social media. Since social media is so visual and quick, we tend to ignore prompts to add text descriptions to photos and other visual media. Make a conscious effort to add text descriptions to photos you share, which often takes mere seconds, and encourage others to do the same. Make this a regular process in the social media activity for group or organizations of which you are a part.

When I share photos of a print book excerpt, I use Google Lens to grab the text, which I then copy-paste into the text description. When using hashtags, capitalize each word to make them readable to a screen reader, which is called camel case (e.g., #MobileMindfulLearning). Favor resharing content that follows these practices. Make sure everyone can enjoy that cat meme and be moved by the words you read. A simple web search will provide more guidance on how to add text descriptions and make social media content accessible.

Recommendations on Social Media for Personal Learning and Growth

- *Patiently wade into social media platforms.* Start with actively engaging in two platforms with which you are familiar and comfortable, and take more of a backseat approach to two other platforms, whether through mostly passive scrolling or reviewing content without an account. Joining one or two Facebook Groups may be convenient if you tend to use Facebook to stay connected with family and friends. Following a few scholars and curated lists on Twitter can help expose you to different perspectives, blogs, podcasts, and other content that does not normally come into your academic purview. If you are on Instagram to follow beautiful photos from your favorite food or travel blogger, check out what educators and scholars might be doing there to reach a larger or more specific public audience. Search the web for top professors of TikTok to browse and compare how they use videos and for what audiences. Bringing curiosity and intention to social media can help reduce the dread associated with social media. Giving a few platforms some time allows you to get a sense of whom you really want to listen to.

- *Follow individual human beings.* Popular publications and organizations tend to repost abundantly from their reporters and journalists, which will inundate your feeds and dilute your experience. Start with following individual human beings, and then add organizations and others sparingly (and don't hesitate to unfollow if it starts to feel like too much noise).

- *Actively listen with reactions and responses.* Online communities thrive when people receive feedback on their content (Lalonde, 2011; Richmond, 2014; Robson, 2018; Roxå & Mårtensson, 2009). Being a good listener and community participant does not have to be very involved, but it puts your name on people's radar.

- *Determine a system for curating content.* You will likely come across good content being shared on social media platforms. How will you save and organize that material? Platforms have their own saving systems (e.g., Twitter bookmarks, Facebook saved posts), but how will they translate beyond the platform? Determine a curation process, whether that is immediately saving links to a note-taking spot on your phone or weekly combing through your saved content and determining how to organize it accordingly.

- *Create boundaries and feedback systems for maintaining healthy social media activity.* When you assessed your phone behavior in chapter 2 you may have reflected on your social media use. If you are the type of person who goes down social media rabbit holes and spends more time in these spaces than feels productive, set boundaries to minimize these effects and have a system for monitoring your activity. If you notice higher levels of stress and anxiety after being on one platform, compare these experiences with other social media platforms and determine how to alter your experience.

- *Consider alternatives to the big platforms.* Using wide, public platforms has a ton of benefits in terms of access to people, information, and collective problem-solving, but many people find they cannot engage on such wide open spaces the way they actually want to. If you have a core group of people with whom you would like to form an online social space, consider social media-esque platforms such as Slack, Mighty Networks, GroupMe, Microsoft Teams, and Discord. Faculty often use both types of spaces: one for a larger stage of idea exchange and networking and another for sharing that feels a bit more secure and private. They may even use public spaces to meet people with similar interests, and then invite those people to one of these more private social online spaces (Moore, 2021).

In chapter 7: Social Learning as a Mobile-Mindful Class, we'll revisit social media with recommendations on integrating these platforms into classes and guiding students.

References

Cavanagh, S. (2020, January 1). Don't resolve to use social media less—Resolve to use it better. *Psychology Today.* https://www.psychologytoday.com/us/blog/once-more-feeling/202001/don-t-resolve-use-social-media-less

Cohn, J. (2021). *Skim, dive, surface: Teaching digital reading.* West Virginia University Press.

Gachago, D., Livingston, C., & Ivala, E. (2016). Podcasts: A technology for all? *British Journal of Educational Technology, 47*(5), 859–872. https://doi.org/10.1111/bjet.12483

Honeycutt, B. (Host). (n.d.). Episode 62: How to use audio lessons in your course to engage students and improve learning with Yehoshua Zlotogorski [Audio podcast episode]. In *Lecture breakers.* https://barbihoneycutt.com/blogs/podcast/episode-62-how-to-use-audio-lessons-in-your-course-to-engage-students-and-improve-learning-with-yehoshua-zlotogorski

Honeycutt, B. (Host). (2022). Episode 112: Learner-centered teaching: Encouraging students to do the work of learning with Dr. Terry Doyle [Audio podcast episode]. In *Lecture breakers.* https://barbihoneycutt.com/blogs/podcast/episode-112-learner-centered-teaching-encouraging-students-to-do-the-work-of-learning-with-dr-terry-doyle

Lalonde, C. (2011). *The Twitter experience: The role of Twitter in the formation and maintenance of personal learning networks* (Publication No. MR75998) [Master's thesis, Royal Roads University]. ProQuest Dissertations Publishing.

Miller, M. D. (2022). *Remembering and forgetting in the age of technology: Teaching, learning, and the science of memory in a wired world.* West Virginia Press.

Moore, C. M. (2021). *How faculty use online social spaces to develop their teaching practices: An ethnographic study of the #ungrading online community* [Dissertation, Oakland University]. ProQuest Dissertations Publishing.

Mueller, P. A., & Oppenheimer, D. M. (2014). The pen is mightier than the keyboard: Advantages of longhand over laptop note taking. *Psychological Science, 25*(6), 1159–1168. https://doi.org/10.1177/0956797614524581

Murray, O. T., & Olcese. N. R. (2011). Teaching and learning with iPads, ready or not? *TechTrends, 55*(6), 42–48. https://link.springer.com/article/10.1007/s11528-011-0540-6

Nave, L. (Host). (2020, June 9). Online faculty learning communities with Christina Moore [Audio podcast episode]. In *ThinkUDL*. https://thinkudl.org/episodes/online-faculty-learning-communities-with-christina-moore

Paul, A. M. (2021). *The extended mind: The power of thinking outside the brain.* Mariner Books.

Richmond, N. (2014). *Digital ethnography: Understanding faculty use of an online community of practice for professional development* (Publication No. 3617808) [Doctoral thesis, Northeastern University]. ProQuest Dissertations Publishing.

Robson, J. (2018). Performance, structure, and ideal identity: Reconceptualising teachers' engagement in online social spaces. *British Journal of Educational Technology, 49*(3), 439–450. https://doi.org/10.1111/bjet.12551

Roxå, T., & Mårtensson, K. (2009). Significant conversations and significant networks—Exploring the backstage of the teaching arena. *Studies in Higher Education, 34*(5), 547–559. https://doi.org/10.1080/03075070802597200

Slack enhances communication for students. (2022, March 30). *OaklandU Online Learning Blog.* https://www.oakland.edu/online/blog/Slack-enhances-communication-for-students

Smydra, R. V. (2022, April). Using podcasts to facilitate learning and skill application in online courses. *ITLC Lilly Online Conference.* https://www.itlclillyonline.com/

Stein, J. (2013, May 20). Millennials: The me me me generation. *Time.* content.time.com

Tamir, D. I., Templeton, E. M., Ward, A. F., & Zaki, J. (2018). Media usage diminishes memory for experiences. *Journal of Experimental Social Psychology, 76,* 161–168. https://doi.org/10.1016/j.jesp.2018.01.006

Wesch, M. (2019, August 23). *10 online teaching tips beyond Zoom: Teaching without walls episode 1* [Video]. YouTube. https://www.youtube.com/watch?v=D7vooDcxUaA

Zlotogorski, Y. (2020, October 30). How to write an audio course. *Alpe Audio Blog.* https://www.alpeaudio.com/post/how-to-write-an-audio-course-%F0%9F%8E%A7/

4

ORGANIZING AND PLANNING MOBILE LEARNING

Once you have observed your phone behaviors, set learning goals, and explored learning in multiple modalities, it's time to channel the right information into the right places and put all of the mobile learning material into action. Making our own mobile-mindful learning successful relies on our ability to rein in information overload: newsletters, social media feeds, books, blogs, discussion boards, journals. Even more complicated is the flow between information: the newsletter that leads us to the blog that leads us to a few articles that lead us to useful tools to try. We need a process for what we do when we recognize something is meaningful, assign it a place and time accordingly, and set up a structure for practicing the material.

Curating Your Learning

Curation is integral to learning, especially in self-led, fluid learning, as "the act of organizing, structuring, and filing helps develop schema for memories and learning" (Hokanson, 2014, p. 52). Curation is the process of organizing material into collections and categories, whether based on action (material to read, videos to watch, and notes to take) or topic (material for a course or an interest area). Furthermore, Deschaine and Sharma's "The Five Cs of Digital Curation" (2015) offers a useful process:

- collect: gathering, describing, cataloging individual items
- categorize: comparing items collected and generalizing them accordingly
- critique: "discriminating, evaluating, and judging the merits of each item" (p. 22)

- conceptualize: applying and connecting the items for new purpose and meaning
- circulation: sharing the results of the four other curation practices

The first two steps of digital curation—collect and categorize—may be most obvious and compatible for mobile learning, but completing the cycle is how new knowledge is created and applied.

We have several decisions to make when we come across useful material on a mobile device: Do we save it in the application where we found it, or save it somewhere else? Do we organize content by topic, mode, project, or something else? While I will offer some suggestions, the curation process needs to be individualized based on your learning preferences, purpose, and mobile behavior. Some people prefer to create a thread on Twitter, rapidly sharing quick comments and links to material related to a theme, tagging people and topics along the way. Others prefer visual organization such as offered on Pinterest. Others might prefer a simple text-based tool such as Google Keep or OneNote, or a robust app specifically for curation (see Appendix B for more curation apps). Following fluid learning principles, whatever system you choose should be easily translatable no matter what device you are using, meaning the same content can be accessed across devices. For example, you won't want to use a note-taking app on your phone that you can't then access on a computer.

Start by taking notice of your current curation practices, or lack thereof. When you come across something useful on your phone that you want to save for a specific purpose, what is your first action? Is that action successful in helping you connect with and apply it at the appropriate time? What works and falls short in this process? Are you content with saving the item with one click, or do you need to add a note on the spot? Prompts like these can help you analyze your curation process and tweak it accordingly with some of the tools and practices mentioned here.

Article and Text-Based Curation Tools

Having a tool that allows you to organize articles in the same place is a must. It should be a tool that can save whatever you are looking at with one or two clicks, whether that is through the Share option on your phone or a web browser extension on your computer ("browser" refers to Google Chrome, Internet Explorer, Apple Safari, etc.). As you will see in "My Mobile-Based Fluid Learning Example" as follows, I started curating my reading with a simple Google Doc. While it worked, it was clumsy to copy a URL, go to that doc, type a title, then hyperlink it. When I shared this process on Twitter, someone recommended using Instapaper, which saves readings in a neutral format. It has been working well for me, but I know there are many other options such as Pocket and Diigo. Using "The Five Cs of Digital Curation" (Deschaine & Sharma, 2015), my current use of Instapaper is good for collection, but from there I tend to use Google Tasks to categorize and critique, where I create a task in the appropriate project list (categorization) and write action items and reading notes (critiquing). Within this note, I write how the piece fits within a current project (conceptualization) and integrate and cite the idea accordingly (circulation).

I do not share my example as an exemplar by any means. There are apps that can do more stages of this curation process than what my current process allows. Nevertheless, this process works and shows that while your curation process may not be perfect, it can still work and be improved over time.

In-App Curation

At times you may find the curation tools within an app to be the most suitable for that material, especially when you are curating media that are not standard text articles. Try subscribing to YouTube channels that align with your learning goals and saving videos to a playlist you create or the Watch Later playlist. Twitter bookmarks are good for saving tweets quickly, such as those with threads of useful ideas, but bookmarks quickly become a list of forgotten things (speaking from experience). Twitter Lists also allow users to curate accounts based on topic, profession, location, or something else, which then channel activity from those accounts in one feed. Audio streaming platforms usually have playlist options for organizing podcasts and music. Pinterest is itself a curation tool, which can be a great tool for mobile learning within and outside of academia (two rhetoric professors, Nichols & Walwema, 2016, used Pinterest to teach digital curation). Since these apps are usually limited to collection and categorization, you will want to determine a process for critiquing, conceptualizing, and circulating the content, such as a weekly routine of reviewing these saved spaces and deleting saved material once it has been processed and integrated accordingly.

Curating Your Ideas

One powerful habit I developed when I "started with self" as a mobile learner was capturing ideas as they came to me rather than hoping I would remember them at a more convenient time. I became more aware of how the brain continues to work in diffuse mode, digesting and interpreting things I had read or listened to in focused mode. In particular, I would be listening to a podcast episode or even just walking and then make a connection to something I had read days or months ago. Developing a mobile note-taking habit was not necessarily about substantive writing but giving myself ideas to work with when I could develop them more in front of a computer.

Photos can be an easy way to capture ideas as you come across them in books, at events, and in different places, but those photos can get lost in a sea of others, such as when your toddler takes a dozen blurry photos of the couch. If you take a photo for learning purposes, take a few more clicks to organize the photo into a relevant album. Better yet, take a note or annotate the actual photo. Taking photos can cause us to remember the object of the photo less than if we hadn't taken the photo at all unless we use the photo-capturing process for deeper analysis (Tamir et al., 2018). This not only organizes your media on your phone but also organizes the idea in your mind, making you more likely to return to that material later and continue to build up that wing of the proverbial "memory palace" mnemonic.

For word-based note-taking, choose an app that is easy to use and, following fluid learning principles, easy to access on any device. Such an app is a good candidate to go on your phone's home screen. If you use Microsoft products, the OneNote app offers many curation and text formatting features. If you tend to work on a Gmail account, Google Keep is easy to access from Gmail and other apps. Google Keep's text formatting features are limited, but include photos and other media. If you favor Apple products across all of your devices, you might prefer Apple Notes or Notability.

You will also want a plan for curating notes for your mobile reading. Apps like Instapaper have note-taking capabilities but are very limited in the free version. Some people find such capabilities worth the extra cost, but otherwise you could have an assigned note-taking space outside of the reading to take notes. You would have to get savvy at going back and forth between readings, which is not too cumbersome as you form new reading routines. For example, If I am confident I will have very few notes or actions to take related to something I am processing, I will use my task manager to create an action item at a relevant time. If I come across a resource I think is important to put in a teaching resource or look into more for a research project, I will click the share icon, share it to my tasks app, and take a few notes on what I want to do with that item and set it for a time when I know I will be able to give it more attention.

End-of-the-Week Digital Review and Cleanup

My mobile learning is more concerned with expediency rather than relevance or organization. It helps to have some organizational procedures in mind to access learning materials on a phone and have an automatic process for saving them, but mobile learning has to be quick and easy. With fluid learning in mind, I find organization and decision-making to be easier to do on a laptop or desktop. Therefore, it is important to periodically organize your mobile learning content, including notes, learning content, and photos. As a part of his Getting Things Done (GTD) system, David Allen ends the week with a review and cleanup, finding a place for every email, letter, and note. At the end of your week, run through your mobile learning storage spots to determine their purpose and where they go accordingly. Organize bookmarked tweets to see what blog posts should be moved to your reading material. Go through your Mobile Junk Drawer to make tasks, put ideas where they go, and get articles into your reading queue.

TIP: SET UP A MOBILE JUNK DRAWER

Having note-curating routines will help you apply more of your mobile learning to other contexts, but you will still find that some moments fall through the cracks. As you listen to a podcast while walking, you may want to take note of something that you heard without taking the time to organize this note. In such cases, planning for the unplanned helps with a Mobile Junk Drawer, which serves as a scratch pad or photo folder and a process for regularly sifting through those materials. The Mobile Junk Drawer also acknowledges our mobile learning in progress: We may not have a perfect mobile learning process for everything, but having an anything-goes space helps in the meantime.

My Mobile Junk Drawer is my personal Slack channel, which is a slightly elevated version of emailing myself. Since I use Slack so frequently, I don't have to think about how to access it. I tend to use this method when I am particularly unplugged, such as on a winter walk, but an idea comes to me that I want to capture and develop more later. Not wanting to click around while wearing gloves, I pull up this channel and use voice-to-text to capture the idea, barely breaking stride in the process. The method could work well if you come across something you want to view later on a larger screen.

TIP: USE VOICE-TO-TEXT TO CAPTURE QUICK THOUGHTS AND LONG RESPONSES

As a developing mobile learner, I found voice-to-text to be a crucial writing practice such as when I am capturing ideas during a walk, curating phone content from the collection phase to critiquing and conceptualization, and digitizing direct quotes from a print book. In all of these writing situations, I have used the microphone icon in the top row of the phone's keyboard. This practice is relatively new for me, and I found that dictation took some getting used to as my thoughts were used to forming words in tandem with the motion of typing or handwriting. Over time, I started to get more used to writing in this way and went from writing a few sentences to a few paragraphs.

RESOURCE HIGHLIGHT: TEACHING AND LEARNING COLLECTIONS AS CURATION EXAMPLE

For curating your own learning, use a note-taking app to organize articles, podcasts, videos, blogs, social media accounts, and other mobile-friendly media based on a topic related to your learning goal. For examples related to teaching topics, see my existing teaching resource collections using the url or QR code (Figure 4.1).

https://oakland.edu/cetl/teaching-resources/

Figure 4.1. QR code for teaching and learning collections as curation example.

These collections are created in Google Docs that invite anyone to make a copy and customize. Delete what is not relevant, reorganize as needed, add more material, and store it somewhere you can easily access on all of your devices. If the previous link changes, you can also visit christinamoorephd.com/MobileMindful.

Recommendations for Mobile-Mindful Curation

- *Choose a few core collecting practices.* As you identify mobile learning content you want to save, organize, and use, determine two or three basic locations and processes. There may be some trial and error, but following consistent practices will help a curation routine stick. While you will want to have a process that works for content from many sources, you might also find it useful to use in-app options (i.e., "Save for Later" features).
- *Map the five Cs of curation: collect, categorize, critique, conceptualize, circulate.* Once you have figured out what your collect-and-save practice will be, complete the curation cycle: Determine apps and features that allow you to organize content based on purpose, analyze these sources,

and ultimately apply and share. Since this is likely a process to span devices, ensure your processes work from phone to computer, and vice versa.

- *Create a Mobile Junk Drawer.* When you have a passing thought, snap a photo, or hear of a book during a podcast and you need to capture it on the spot, have a place to curate things later. This Mobile Junk Drawer should be in a space that can be easily accessed on a computer since its primary purpose is to access the content later in a more focused, developed way.
- *Develop a routine for cumulative curation.* If you have multiple curation locations and strategies, regularly set aside time to process all of these locations: notes, in-app saved content, and the Mobile Junk Drawer.

Retrieval Practice and Memory

Some learning goals benefit from having a massive bank of memorized facts from which to draw. After justified criticism of rote memorization and "drill-and-kill" educational tactics, educational psychologists and neuroscience of learning experts are reminding us that memorization and recall are not automatically futile learning tasks. As cognitive psychologist Michelle D. Miller (2022) argued in her work on memory and learning, memory still has an important role in the world of search engines and ubiquitous knowledge. It is when we intentionally memorize to serve more complex learning concepts that memory becomes powerful. Holding key facts in our heads allows us to uniquely assemble this knowledge for our current problems and curiosities. Relating it to Bloom's taxonomy, higher order thinking skills often require lower thinking skills. Consider what learning goal you might have that is significantly bolstered by memory and recall, whether it is something discipline-based, related to learning theories, or for your personal enrichment.

Phone-based flashcards are convenient, adaptable, sharable, and expansive. Anki and Quizlet are two popular, well-established flashcard apps. If you engage in a project related to course content, you will be able to share that deck with students. Figure 4.2 is an example of an Anki flashcard from a biochemistry set I downloaded from Shared Decks. This 141-card set presents 20 cards in one session and consists of text and sometimes images with fill-in-the-blanks. Upon revealing the answer (peroxisomes), Anki gives you options on when it will ask you this question again, HARD meaning since it was difficult it may give you this card again sooner than others you rate

Figure 4.2. Screenshot of a mobile flashcard with a biochemistry question in the Anki app.

8:00 🔲 🔇   🔇 📶 📶 59% 🔋

≡   **Biochemistry**   ↩   ⚑   ⋮
     7 minutes left

<u>20</u> 0 0

__ are membrane-bound packets of **oxidative enzymes.**

In **plant cells**, they play a variety of roles including **converting fatty acids to sugar and assisting chloroplasts in photorespiration.**

In animal cells, they **protect the cell from its own production of toxic hydrogen peroxide**.

peroxisomes

< 1 min	< 6 min	< 10 min	4 d
AGAIN	HARD	GOOD	EASY

III   O   <

GOOD or EASY. Your results will determine what cards may come in the next 20-card set.

To encourage her biology students to engage in distributed retrieval practice rather than cramming, Kelly Thomasson from University of California Santa Barbara used Snapchat to post a few photos of vertebrate animals daily, which prompted students to identify the animal by text. Her students liked it so much they asked her for more (Rockey et al., 2019).

That being said, since I have preached that "mobile" can also be no-tech print materials, physical flashcards may provide a tactile experience that is helpful to memory if you are up for carrying them around. (You could also take photos of these cards as a digital backup.) Cognitive psychologist and neuroscientist Daniel Levintin (2015) advocated for tactile flashcards in his book, *The Organized Mind: Thinking Straight in the Age of Information Overload.* We'll explore more on retrieval practice in chapter 8: Dive Into Mobile-First Opportunities.

Executive Functions With Reminders and Tasks

When I signed the contract for this book, I would start my dissertation study exactly a month later. Exciting, but overwhelming. I had to plan not only for how to stay focused on my projects but also how to keep up my energy by moving my body away from the desktop. Less than directly about mobile learning, attending to mobile methods for executive functions sets the pathways for learning to happen.

Executive functions, or capabilities that allow us to plan and organize our actions, are where mobile notifications can be used to return our focus rather than distract. Using reminder or task apps, we can enable notifications to tell us when to get up and move, when to pack a bag for the next day, and when to spend 15 minutes flipping through flashcards or chipping away at a reading. By planning these actions out for the appropriate place and time, our brain is free of ambient worry that we are forgetting something or not spending our time properly. In other words, when the miscellaneous, smaller, routine actions are planned, our brain has the freedom to stay focused on the task at hand or to do nothing.

Phones can also remind us to be mobile learners if we use its distracting vices as virtues. Phones are designed to be distracting with notifications, alluring colors and light, and attention-grabbing content, all of which tax our executive functions. Executive functions refer to the brain's ability to plan and organize, which includes regulating our attention, prioritizing information, and making decisions accordingly. Our brain is not great at holding many different concepts in its short-term memory at the same time, so we are easily distracted and prone to task switching (the more appropriate phrase since we can only multitask under specific conditions). To compensate for this, our executive functions might involve planning a task list and determining which thoughts require immediate action and which can be attended to at a later time.

When we teach students to be mobile-mindful learners, we can get double points by teaching students to mute unwanted notifications and increase beneficial notifications. As the Center for Humane Technology (2021) recommends, turn off any notifications that are not direct communications from humans you know who require your immediate attention. Then, set a daily reminder to answer five practice questions and flip through flashcards. Also, use notifications from the apps directly, if possible, as a click will likely take you right to the desired content. Otherwise, use Google Tasks or some other mobile task list to prompt behavior. This nudging will only work if distracting notifications are muted; otherwise, you are more likely to be pulled away by other notifications that provide more instant gratification.

Notifications: Sifting Out and Reining In

Every time a notification comes through on your phone, consider not only whether you want to be notified, but also how often you want to be notified. Do you want a push notification four times an hour with the newest breaking story from CNN or a daily digest? When you receive a notification, hold down that notification, which will usually yield options such as showing the notification silently or not showing them at all. Notifications from a messaging platform like Slack or Discord may allow you to customize when you want to pause notifications or when you want to be displayed as "available" to others in the space. You may decide that you do not mind some notifications, such as pictures from your child's daycare. Once you sift out the noise and your brain does not have to evaluate the relevance of every buzz and ping, you can rein in the notifications you want to receive for your own learning and enjoyment.

Reminders Versus Tasks

I've grown to appreciate the distinction between reminders and tasks. Reminders are things I need to think about or do at a set time and place; therefore, I want them to pop up on my phone since it is likely to be with me. Reminders are fleeting: I can either dismiss them right away once I've recognized the message, or I will want to act on something right away. However, tasks don't work this way in my work and lifeflow. Tasks are the things I sit down to do, usually involving my computer or a smaller part of a work project. Since tasks are likely to be attended to on a computer, I do not have task notifications come to my phone. There are many robust task managers with tags, labels, and the like, such as Todoist, but for now I stick with simple Google Reminders and Tasks, which I can create and arrange within Google Calendar.

My Mobile-Based Fluid Learning Example

As I moved to intentional mobile-mindful learning, I analyzed how my learning flowed among devices (fluid learning) and spaces (learning ecologies). Fluid learning is being able to carry out a learning activity across devices, time, and space seamlessly (Fang, 2014). Fluid learning is defined by five characteristics:

- neutrality: works well on any device
- granularity: can be consumed in smaller units
- portability: used across platforms
- interactivity: potential connection among others
- ubiquity: learning beyond devices, existing everywhere

Learning ecologies (Barron, 2006) acknowledge learning that occurs across formal (i.e., education institution), nonformal (organized, but not for accreditation or certification), and informal (everyday, unplanned or organized) spaces. The four following screenshots (see Figures 4.3–4.6) show how I engaged in mobile learning and which of Fang's fluid learning characteristics were in action.

Part 1: Reading on the Go List

- app: Google Docs
- fluid learning characteristic: portable, neutral
- learning ecology realm: informal

The first example is a "Reading on the Go" Google Doc I started on my desktop. In my resolution to capitalize on mobile learning, I started saving articles of interest that I would normally let pass through social media feeds and newsletters. When I saw an article of interest that I didn't have time to read at that moment, I would pull up this Reading on the Go doc and hyperlink the title. I also kept a Done category where I moved titles once I was done reading them. Google Docs can be accessed easily from multiple locations (portable) and scales well to any device (neutral).

Figure 4.3. Phone screenshot of fluid learning example: curating articles in Google Docs.

Reading on the Go

- How I Wrote a Book While Working a 9-to-5 Job
- Using Structure for Inclusive Teaching (Elon University)
- An Elite STEM College Makes Conflict Resolution Lesson 1
- The Power of Dialogue: Consequences of Intergroup Dialogue and their Implications for Agency and Alliance Building
- Achievement Gap Closed
- The Case for Reparations

Done

- Centers of the Pedagogical Universe
- Decorative neuroscience: Expertise, communication and the problem of keynoting with translational science

Parts 2 and 3: Sharing the Idea on Social Media

- app: Twitter
- fluid learning characteristics: ubiquitous, interactive
- learning ecology realm: nonformal

I was part of an online un-book club that talked about goals related to reading about higher education. I figured my Reading on the Go strategy might be useful to others in the group, so I briefly shared on Twitter my process and a screenshot as an example with the hashtag #HigherEdReads (hashtags curate tweets around a topic, group, or discussion).

Figure 4.4. Phone screenshot of fluid learning example: sharing mobile learning process on Twitter.

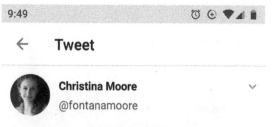
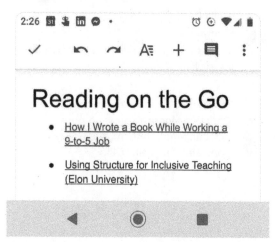

By posting my idea to social media, others could comment on the idea that I shared. One person suggested an app that organizes content well called Instapaper. She explained that Instapaper curates the content with a single click from a browser plugin.

Figure 4.5. Phone screenshot of fluid learning example: response on Twitter leading to new curation app.

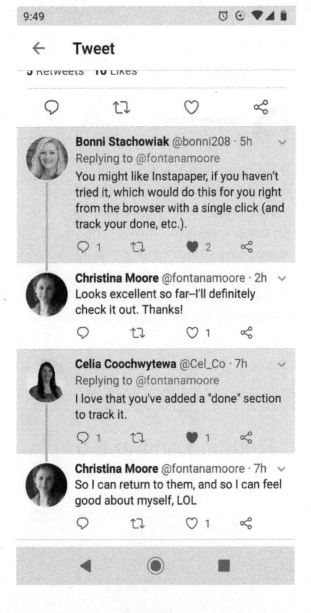

By making my learning moment social and interactive, I learned how to make my learning even more accessible.

Figure 4.6. Phone screenshot of fluid learning example: Instapaper curating articles.

Part 4: Curating and Reading With Instapaper

- app: Instapaper
- fluid learning characteristics: granular, portable, neutral
- learning ecology realm: informal

Instapaper ended up being a huge improvement to my original Google Doc. Wherever I opened the article, I could share it to Instapaper in one click. Then, the app organized the reading material and neutralized the content of any odd formatting. If you leave an article and come back to it later, it will automatically scroll to the place where you left off, which adds a "granular" element to mobile learning.

The more mobile-mindful you become, the longer this learning flow continues. The type of activity I show in this example continues to flow into formal realms of my learning ecology such as work projects, presentations, and this book. With fewer barriers to learning and process on how to curate your learning, you get so much out of your experiences.

In Review: How to Be a Mobile-Mindful Learner

This section explained some mobile-mindful learning basics with the encouragement to try these out for yourself to see what kind of mobile learner you are and could become. Now that you have read through explanations, examples, tools, and tips, let's review the seven main actions and considerations in being a mobile-mindful learner:

1. *Draw a mobile learning portrait by accounting for your material and environmental learning conditions.* Where do you tend to work and learn? In what environment do you feel the most energized and motivated to work and learn? As you move throughout your day, reflect on which times, spaces, and movements could be conducive to mobile learning. Where do you experience barriers to learning? Paying attention to where you learn well, what hinders learning, and how you would like to engage in mobile learning if you had better tools or skills can help guide the rest of your mobile learning actions and goals.

2. *Try reading in multiple formats.* When do you read in print, on a computer, and on a phone? Consider a process for strategically using each of these modes and determine ways to connect them, such as taking digital notes while print reading or using programs that allow you to pick up

reading on a computer or phone. In your digital reading, hone annotation and note-taking that works across devices, whether within tools such as Kindle books or in note-taking apps.

3. *Branch beyond alphabetic reading by learning through audio and visual formats.* Consider the best ways to leverage audio formats such as audio books, podcasts, and other audio files. With the convenience of audio learning comes the tendency toward passive learning: Therefore, build in ways to interact with audio content such as taking the "podcast pause" to note important points and take notes. Audio courses are mindful of learning structures by building in key points, prompting, audio cues, and retrieval practice. Engage in audio courses to compare the learning experiences to other audio content. Similarly, recognize the variety of visual media that can contribute to learning such as videos, infographics, photos, slide decks, and maps.

4. *Use phones to engage in social learning or learning through and with people.* Social media platforms allow us to easily ask questions of our networks or to tap into the ideas others are sharing. Even if we have some hesitation about social media, we can employ practices that maximize its benefits and minimize its risks. Additionally, you can create private online social spaces for tighter knit communities of learners.

5. *Organize your mobile learning, and channel the flow of content and ideas across modes and devices.* Come up with a process for saving and applying content, which may involve in-app curation such as those in social media accounts or may use apps that channel content from many different sources. Practice ways to quickly capture your ideas, such as a note-taking app, and come up with a process for ensuring those notes make it to their intended destination. Even if you have a streamlined system, plan a Mobile Junk Drawer where you will store things when you don't have time to identify the right place it, which might be a random note pinned to your phone's home screen or even your photo album. Then regularly apply this data through a daily or weekly digital review and cleanup, combing through in-app saved material, notes, and the junk drawer.

6. *Increase opportunities for recalling and applying small concepts as a foundation for larger thinking.* The more often we engage in retrieval practice, the more effectively we encode concepts. Memorizing and practicing with flashcard-sized content helps us achieve an expansive breadth and depth to our learning, and smartphones are perfect for this type of learning.

Embrace online flashcards that are not only convenient but can track your performance, randomize cards, and grow through collaboration.

7. *Use a phone's distraction vices for executive function virtues.* Adjust notifications to eliminate or condense unwanted notifications and set notifications to remind you to practice a skill, consult a source, and overall keep you on track toward your goals. Aside from notifications, use mobile task lists to fit ideas, resources, and actions into your large projects.

What Now?

More than building up your mobile learning skills to be a more productive scholar or checking off tasks, I hope honing these habits helps you achieve a learning flow that feeds your curiosity and creativity. Using the tools, activities, examples, and recommendations offered in this section, figure out how mobile-mindful learning could help you increase your learning goals. Start planning how you can create fluid learning opportunities that get the most out of those mobile moments when you are in the waiting room or preparing a meal. If you know you need to be walking outside more often, complement it with a podcast. Your mobile-mindful learning goals can be for those topics too often neglected, such as a hobby or a skill completely unrelated to your profession. Learning about something brand new might also be a great experiment, as you are more likely to see the before-and-after results.

Part of being mobile-mindful is not just engaging with the screen more, but also monitoring your mobile habits. Sometimes you will easily maintain healthy mobile and nonsmartphone boundaries while at other times you will feel yourself sliding into unproductive phone behaviors. The goal is to simply notice what is happening and tip the scale back toward intentional use, which might include limiting social media use or checking your phone's screen time or digital wellbeing app for how long your phone is unlocked daily. Over time, assess your mobile learning strategy: Are you achieving your goals? How do you feel about your mobile learning? What type of mobile learning strategies are working best for you, and which are not bringing benefits? Then reflect on how your mobile-mindful learning experiences can be translated into mobile-mindful teaching opportunities.

References

Barron, B. (2006). Interest and self-sustained learning as catalysts of development: A learning ecologies perspective. *Human Development, 49*(4), 193–224. http://dx.doi.org/10.1159%2F000094368

Center for Humane Technology. (2021). *Take control.* humanetech.com/take-control

Deschaine, M. E., & Sharma, S. A. (2015). The five Cs of digital curation: Supporting twenty-first-century teaching and learning. *InSight: A Journal of Scholarly Teaching, 10*(1), 19–24. https://eric.ed.gov/?id=EJ1074044

Fang, B. (2014, October 13). Creating a fluid learning environment. *EDUCAUSE Review.* https://er.educause.edu/articles/2014/10/creating-a-fluid-learning-environment

Hokanson, B. (2014). Rich and remote learning and cognition: Analog methods as models for newer technology. In C. Miller & A. Doering (Eds.), *The new landscape of mobile learning* (pp. 42–55). Routledge.

Levintin, D. L. (2015). *The organized mind: Thinking straight in the age of information overload.* Dutton.

Miller, M. D. (2022). *Remembering and forgetting in the age of technology: Teaching, learning, and the science of memory in a wired world.* West Virginia Press.

Nichols, R. D, & Walwema, J. (2016). Untangling the web through digital aggregation and curation. In C. Lutkewitte (Ed.), *Mobile technologies and the writing classroom: Resources for teachers* (pp. 194–206). National Council of Teachers of English.

Rockey, A., Eastman, S., Colin, M., & Merrill, M. (2019). Spotlighting innovative use cases of mobile learning. *The Emerging Learning Design Journal, 6*(1), 13–15. https://digitalcommons.montclair.edu/eldj/vol6/iss1/3/

Tamir, D. I., Templeton, E. M., Ward, A. F., & Zaki, J. (2018). Media usage diminishes memory for experiences. *Journal of Experimental Social Psychology, 76,* 161–168. https://doi.org/10.1016/j.jesp.2018.01.006

PART TWO

TOWARD MOBILE-MINDFUL TEACHING

Chapters 2–4 familiarized us with key mobile-mindful learning actions, including how to consume and curate content and create mobile learning processes through activities and task management. With these skills and a familiarity with many mobile learning functions, we can be more prepared to think about how to leverage phones to increase and deepen student learning related to our courses.

After diving deeper into mobile-mindful learning, I hope you see opportunities for mobile-mindful learning in your courses. You may have many links, resources, and ideas, so now it is time to think about how to start introducing mobile-mindful learning possibilities without overwhelming students and yourself. You might eventually even dabble in "mobile-first" learning materials designed with phones in mind, such as slide decks made to phone dimensions and interactive maps. The recommendations in this section of the book provide a possible sequence of teaching actions, but do not need to be approached in exactly this order. Gradually and sustainably introducing mobile-mindful teaching and learning is key.

5

PREPARE COURSES FOR
MOBILE LEARNING

Preparing courses for mobile learning can seem like an overwhelming task. These suggestions favor a slow approach, starting by simply observing how your course functions on a phone, from course materials and activities to the LMS. From there, we'll plan for how technology functions during live class sessions, observing how technologies are currently used and planning for intentional use. As you start identifying good opportunities to use apps and other mobile technologies, we will pause to evaluate ethical considerations surrounding technology choices such as hardware access, privacy and data sharing, taxes on attention, and digital accessibility. With a plan in place, it's time to bring in key players, such as the tech experts who will be able to make your vision a reality. With mobile-mindful options ready, bring students into the process, as they will need guidance on how to take advantage of mobile-mindful learning options. Decide together how class social learning spaces will work. As mobile-mindful teaching and learning gain traction, you may even start exploring more mobile-first activities that best take advantage of mobile learning's affordances.

Take a Mobile Test Drive Through the Course

Walk through the syllabus, LMS, or wherever you communicate and keep course texts, activities, and student work, and evaluate how these materials function on a mobile device.

- What already works well, and what does not?
- Which activities would be useful for mobile access, such as those for granular, frequent access?

- Which activities are not ideal for mobile tech, such as materials that are more complex and expansive?
- Consider how course content can be made more mobile, both in terms of learning on and captured by smartphones. The fluid analysis course planning activity in chapter 10 guides you through identifying which devices can be used to access course materials, along with space to explain why access might be limited and brainstorm ways to increase options. While you could go through your syllabus to review learning materials, you'll likely get the most informative experience going through the place where you house those learning materials, especially in the LMS.

Mobile Learning on the LMS

Back in January 2020 (two months before the COVID-19 pandemic hit most of the world in earnest), nearly 29% of access to Moodle at my university was on a mobile device. About half of these mobile users used a web browser (e.g., Google Chrome, Internet Explorer, Apple Safari) while the other half used the Moodle mobile app. LMS are standard at most universities and serve as an online course space for individual classes. While often the central hub for online courses, they are increasingly used for any course regardless of modality as a place to share resources, create activities, keep records, and communicate. While some institutions automatically assign an LMS page for every course, others might require faculty to request one. Common LMS options include Canvas, Moodle, and Blackboard, among others.

If you use the LMS, practice accessing your course on your phone:

1. How would you get to your course page? Can you access it through an app?
2. What type of learning materials (readings, slides, videos) are viewable, and with what amount of ease?
3. What kind of learning activity could a student complete on a phone, and to what extent?

It is likely your students are accessing the LMS from their phones more often than you would guess and will try to complete any activity even if, to you, it is clearly not accessible on a phone. LMS support staff may be able to show you how to get an accurate idea of how students are accessing course resources and activities. Additionally, it is worth walking through all of the activities to understand what issues students might encounter with them.

From there you can provide guidance on how students should and should not access course content from their phones. Resist saying students should *never* access the course on their phones, as some simple functions may be good to include on a phone such as checking grades, communication, and taking simple quizzes.

I accessed a graduate course I took as a student from my Android smartphone to test the usability of the course materials, both through the Moodle LMS app and via mobile web browser. I was surprised to find how well both the app and the browser scaled the course material, as I found the course navigable and much of the content readable on both. Of course, some materials were not fully accessible, such as the narrated PowerPoint slides which were used as the main lecture material. While I could view the slides and see there was an audio icon, I could not figure out how to actually play the audio. It may be possible if I download the PowerPoint app, but I figure most students would not go to these pains. Many other learning materials such as Word docs, PDFs, and videos were readable, even PDFs with photos. Only Word docs with more complex formatting like tables did not always display all of the information in the cells.

The mobile app was overall clearer and more usable for completing activities such as forum discussions. Maybe most importantly, students can receive phone notifications whenever the instructor sends an announcement or grades an item, which they will acknowledge and attend to more quickly than when receiving an email notification. The only downside to the mobile app is that it did not clearly provide the multiple mode options available in Blackboard Ally, an accessibility tool our institution adopted. When I accessed the course through the browser, I could see the Blackboard Ally-enabled format options. From the instructor side, Blackboard Ally assesses the accessibility of anything uploaded to the LMS and offers ways to remediate the content accordingly. From the student side, the tool automatically offers course content in multiple formats such as audio, tagged PDF, and eBraille.

While the usability of the LMS app should inform your course activities and how you explain them to students, it is fair to acknowledge that some actions are not compatible with phones. The mobile LMS is difficult when doing more complex actions, such as taking tests or attaching files. While one could write long posts in a forum, especially if they use voice-to-text, it could be clunky if the forum activity requires citations and links. Explain to students that their phones are great for the work leading up to these complex activities, such as capturing their initial ideas for a longer writing piece, flipping through flashcards, and making a task list or plan for preparing for these projects. The more preliminary work they do on their phones, the more efficiently they can use their time completing these tasks on a computer. On this note, your pedagogical purpose matters: If small, frequent quizzes are meant to help students with retrieval practice leading up to a larger assessment, these may be worth doing in a mobile friendly format, where students are more likely to be able to engage with short learning activities multiple times.

While there are likely to be similar experiences across different LMS, walking through your own course materials on the LMS will be informative and produce different results and realizations. We can help students fully use their mobile learning options by evaluating how much of our course is mobile accessible, considering how to increase this accessibility, and communicating these options to students. If your LMS allows for it, you can view the course from a student role, both on a phone's web browser and mobile app. As we'll soon explore in more depth, partnering with students is crucial: The LMS mobile access data from my institution showed that half of those accessing the LMS on their phones were using the browser, likely because they didn't know there was an app version. By giving them a clearer sense of what learning actions are better suited for phones, such as reading articles or watching videos, they can make the best use of time when they are sitting in front of a computer to complete more complex activities.

Create and Select "Neutral" Modes of Content

A neutral format means the format is not specific to a type of device and, therefore, will scale well to different screen sizes and device types. Web content from popular venues such as YouTube, Google products, and others are designed to scale to different devices. As you update syllabi leading up to a new semester, check how course items scale, load, and interact on a smartphone. If there is more than one version of the same course text, opt for the one that works well on multiple devices, or offer multiple options. For example, if your course materials include news stories, consider that American adults of all ages consume news on their phones more than any other mode (Walker, 2019). By ensuring your news links scale well to mobile devices, you will be tapping into an information habit students are more likely to have.

When it comes to content that you create, such as the syllabus and assignment descriptions, create and share these in a format friendly to all devices and that encourages student engagement. By sharing the syllabus in a Google Doc or Microsoft Word doc, students can not only access it on multiple devices, but annotate it according to their needs, although they would need the app to open it. (Note: While Microsoft Word is a paid program, phones will often offer a free edit or view option through programs like Google Drive.) By putting reminders and announcements through an LMS forum, students will get a notification on their phone if the LMS has an app and students are prompted to download it. By uploading an instructional video to YouTube, students can view it on the spot or add it to a Watch Later playlist. Even better, when you curate a YouTube playlist for the course, students are more likely to keep viewing and watch videos more than once.

TIP: EMULATE A MOBILE DEVICE IN A DESKTOP BROWSER

The experience of clicking through course materials on a phone is useful, but you can also see how web content would look on a phone right from your web browser using the browser's developer tools. Developer tools is a menu option in any browser, or will open with the keyboard shortcut Ctrl + Shift + I (for Mac, Command + Option + I), where the top bar will show a two-rectangle icon typically used to preview how pages look on a mobile device. It will even allow you to see how links will open and display content. Sometimes resizing browser windows to be narrower like a phone can give you a preview of how pages look on a phone. This method is good for a first look, especially when focusing on webpages, but won't be effective for content that would normally be opened with an app. For example, a Google Doc will not scale well in this emulator because Google Docs would commonly be viewed with the Google Docs app, which will display a Google Doc properly.

Plan Frequent Retrieval Practice

Mobile devices are perfect for implementing key learning actions such as distributed practice (practicing over time) and interleaved practice (different types of thinking activities in one study session), but our courses tend to provide limited opportunities to engage in this type of learning activity. As you become more mobile-mindful, consider ways to use phones to engage students with the material in small, systematic ways dozens of times with a few taps on their phones.

Let's start with a simple exercise: Identify three concepts that are foundational to your course. Then, reflect on how your students come into contact with these concepts in your course:

- When are students introduced to this concept?
- How often are students prompted to recall or use this concept, and over how much time?

- How do students know if they know these concepts? (In other words, are they given the chance to receive feedback, whether via quiz answers or student responses?)

As experts in our fields, we may think these foundational concepts are a given, even if we aren't always explicitly pointing back to the vocabulary and definitions as they relate to other content. But novices do not always have the ability to see how concepts relate to one another. Mobile-mindful teaching and learning increases the frequency with which students recall, test, and apply these concepts. Start with these three concepts, and trace how often students are prompted to work with these concepts at different thinking levels such as those proposed in Bloom's taxonomy: define a theory, compare theories, evaluate errors in a case study using these theories, and so forth. The more opportunities they have to explicitly work with course concepts, the better prepared they will be to know when to apply them.

Example: Rhetorical Appeals

When I teach an introductory composition course, one course learning outcome is defining, distinguishing, and applying rhetorical appeals, the main four being logos (appeal to logic), pathos (appeal to emotion), ethos (appeal to character, value system), and kairos (appeal to context and situation). I might introduce rhetorical appeals in the first couple of weeks with direct instruction, class activities, and individual assignments, but only mention the concept as it comes up in the following 8 weeks and then expect students to demonstrate a strong understanding for the final project. Taking a mobile learning approach, I would do the following:

- Search for premade flashcards on Quizlet related to rhetorical appeals. Flashcard collections will likely have more definitions, which allow students to bump up against other important terms.
- Ask students for examples of each rhetorical appeal from pop culture, politics, history, and literature, and use these examples to make quizzes in Google Forms or Quizlet. If students do this in teams, one team could even do "quality control" for these examples and create the actual quizzes.
- Charge students with finding good and bad explanations of these rhetorical appeals (YouTube videos, blogs, etc.). For example, in the past my students have referred to examples from Pinterest of logos, pathos, and ethos (one consisted of matching Harry Potter characters to each appeal), which could provide good conversation starters about the validity of these examples.

See the Wrap the Class Session With Short Surveys teaching activity in chapter 11 for related examples and ideas.

Consider the Flow of Tech Use in the Classroom

So far we have thought about how students access technology to learn at their own pace and place, especially when it comes to reading, instruction, review, and response activities. Concentrating mobile-mindful learning outside of class time sidesteps the frustration faculty may face with tech distraction in the classroom. Some faculty ban the use of technology in their classes, intentionally implement the tech students have into class activities, or leave it to students to choose what they do.

I understand the dread we feel about students constantly shifting focus to screens and away from the humans in the classroom. We have so little time together in on-campus or synchronous online sessions, and these are opportune times to build community and understanding. The approach José Bowen advocates for in *Teaching Naked* might be a useful starting point: While tech can distract students from one another when they are in the same space, the tech keeps students connected when they are not in the same space. This being said, we can take different approaches to how we implement tech use in the classroom without banning technology outright, which disproportionately disadvantages women, students of color, disabled students, and lower-income students who rely on tech-based resources to succeed at a higher rate than other groups (Galanek et al., 2018).

As James Lang (2020) offered in *Distracted: Why Students Can't Focus and What You Can Do About It*, it may be more beneficial to consider what parts of class are appropriate to request students refrain from screens and when students might be encouraged to use them. Offering students the option to use their phones for polling or to otherwise gather feedback can draw their attention back to the course, but admittedly it could also draw students' attention away if a notification is waiting for them on their phones. Without outright banning phones and other technology in the classroom, you can discuss with students what use of technology is most conducive to their learning, provide concrete recommendations, and make these practices explicit in the syllabus (more in the Mobile-Mindful Syllabus course planning activity). Especially early in the process of implementing more mobile learning activities, get student input on what works well for them and concerns they have. Students might encourage the instructor to give cues on when to "unplug" from laptops and phones to connect to a whole-class experience for 10 minutes, while not strictly forcing students to put their devices out of sight. They might find that so much of class time is engaged actively with one another through case study discussions or lab work that phone distraction isn't a problem. Small classes engaging in whole-class discussion may want to try having totally unplugged classes, save a 10-minute anything-goes break. When talking with students about recommended situations for using and refraining from using their phones in class, we recognize attention as the flow of different activities.

Print: Flow to and Away From Digital Modes

Yes, even in our mobile-mindful efforts we should consider how to also include print media options in the learning flow of the course. Students themselves might appreciate a break from the screen, especially if they have frustratingly slow devices or find them challenging to use for learning tasks. Print pages won't have social media notifications pop in view or disappear unexpectedly. Print is the mode you can count on if you have access to a printer. Even in print work, consider how to link it to mobile as needed. Add QR codes and shortened URLs via bit.ly and tinyurl to print versions of a course item. Creating and using QR codes has become increasingly simple. In many web browsers, the URL bar has a one-click option to create a QR code for whatever page you are on (sometimes two clicks: starting with the share icon, with QR code being one option). From there you download the QR code image and stick it onto your page. Scanning QR codes is also standard from a smartphone's camera: Simply pointing the camera at a QR code will show a URL that someone can click to access the source page.

TIP: KEEP A FEW PRINTOUTS ON HAND

As a writing instructor, I designed hybrid courses so that we were mostly working on devices even when we were on campus, as my classroom's internet access was reliable and enough students had laptops to facilitate small group activities. Still, in the interest of fluid learning principles, I tried to keep at least a few print copies of activities and articles on hand for students who needed or preferred them, particularly since I had access to printing services through my academic department. Regardless of age, some students find they focus better with a print copy in front of them and may want to write by hand. I like to offer print copies of articles, especially when they are longer with formats less friendly for mobile devices.

Gather Timely Student Feedback During Class Sessions

Using phones as audience response systems (i.e., "clickers") or ways to get quick answers from students during a class session is one of the most common mobile learning moves I have encountered in the literature and in conversations with faculty. It is easy to see the appeal as students have the technology with them, they can answer simple questions, and everyone can see the data instantaneously. You may have even experienced such activities as a conference participant or in another group learning environment. Whatever app or program you use, the overall process will likely be the same: Plan questions and create the questions ahead of class time, display how students can get to the questions, and then display and discuss the data.

While there are countless ways to use mobile-friendly response systems in class, these are a few places to start:

- *Ask review questions at the beginning of class.* To focus students' attention toward class, pose a few questions that prompt students to recall concepts from the previous class session and their homework. Even better, choose questions that show a connection between previous content and upcoming course content.

- *Ask priming questions before students have the knowledge.* According to Kolb's (1984) experiential learning cycle, learning can have more impact if students are asked about content they have not yet learned formally (i.e., haven't received instruction or done the reading). By answering such questions, students can see what they did and did not know about the subject before the learning experience. You can also start the discussion with students' answers, pointing out what they know and don't know, or questions that have resulted in split decisions. Additionally, you can then ask them the same questions at a later period so they can see how their knowledge has changed.

- *Work on a question multiple times.* Ask students a multiple-choice question in class that they answer individually, preferably a tough question. Show the results, and then have students discuss the question in small groups. After these discussions, have each student answer the same question again to see if responses change. Discuss this question as a whole class and pose the question one more time.

- *Gather data about students.* Asking simple questions about students' experiences can be a powerful way to make course content relevant to students, either as a class opener or to refocus students midway through a session. Such an activity could also be done asynchronously and then discussed in an instructional video or other medium. Questions pertaining to identity could be powerful as well, but these questions should be planned out with care to ensure anonymous results do not unintentionally exclude students or out them as one or a few of a certain identity group.

- *Ask "temperature check" questions.* These types of questions can be used multiple times throughout the semester to check on students' understanding of a topic or preparedness for a task. Asking them scaled questions about how well they understand the lesson or how prepared they feel for an exam can help you quickly get a sense of what content needs more clarification.
- *Collect exit tickets.* Exit tickets have been used to conclude a class session in a learning move that helps the brain process and effectively situate new knowledge with prior knowledge. Different strategies include the "one-minute essay" or "muddiest point," and doing these on a phone can make their collection, review, curation, and application more effective.

Poll Everywhere, Mentimeter, and Kahoot have long been used to have students answer different question types, from multiple choice to open answer. They do not require an app: Students instead go to a weblink and enter a code. Share the weblink by displaying the URL and using a QR code for a quick scan off the projector. These "freemium" (limited free version with paid premium options) programs tend to be limited in the number of responses they can receive or questions they can ask. Many mobile- and computer-friendly survey tools can be used for this purpose as well, such as Google Forms, Qualtrics, or Survey Monkey.

Ethical Considerations Around Mobile Technology Use

So far, we have evaluated the current mobile-readiness of our courses, identifying what works well on mobile and where there is opportunity for increased access. We have used this data to start imagining how mobile devices could be used during and between class periods. We may have already begun planning small changes to our courses, such as adding recommended apps in the syllabus and ways to talk with students about mobile-mindful learning. Whenever we encourage or require students to use a technology, we should pause to evaluate the ethics surrounding that technology. This pause goes for any new technology, but especially mobile technology since it is so ubiquitous and yet unfamiliar in the educational terrain. It is one thing to pick and choose mobile learning actions for ourselves and another thing to direct students into certain tech uses.

These guidelines are not meant to be barriers to embracing mobile-mindful learning. In fact, they are opportunities to help students better understand and control their smartphone use in all contexts. Tending to these ethical issues with students is "a matter of helping them to understand

and be able to assess—to pay attention to—the social, economic, and peda-gogical implications of new communication technologies and technological initiatives that affect their lives" (Selfe, 1999, p. 432). When actively using mobile tech with students, we must always ask, "What are we signing them up for? (Ultimately, we must get them to ask that question themselves and take it with them)" (Gilliard, 2017, para. 10). To avoid adding a unit to your course on digital citizenship, approach ethics broadly, making students aware of mobile-mindful learning conditions such as privacy, bandwidth, and the reciprocity taking place with using learning technology. From there, we can allow space for students to dig into these ethical considerations through assignments and other research activities such as the ideas offered in chapter 11.

When you use a fluid learning design, activities are "mobile-supported" rather than "mobile-dependent," meaning students can opt out of using mobile apps at any time (Dennen & Hao, 2014, p. 403). If an activity is mobile-dependent, explain why the use of a mobile phone and app is integral to the learning goal and make students aware of what conditions come with using the app. You could also design the learning activity so that students not using a phone can partner with someone who is. By being mindful of broader ethical issues, making mobile-mindful teaching choices accordingly, communicating those choices with students, and guiding them toward how to make their own choices, we can increase mobile learning access in a way that acknowledges our students' material and cultural contexts.

Hardware Access

As long as politicians and other leaders have touted technology advances as a great class equalizer, tech has been distributed and adopted unevenly across socioeconomic status, with students in lower class areas having less access to reliable technology and internet access (Selfe, 1999; Pew Research Center, 2019). Encouragingly, the gap in tech ownership by class and race is clos-ing (Pew Research Center, 2021), but significant inequities remain. Even if our students are likely to have both a phone and a personal computer, people in a lower socioeconomic status are more likely to experience unreli-able internet access and are generally more likely to rely on their phones to access the internet. While broadband internet access is increasing, 30% of all Americans said they experience connectivity issues (Perrin, 2021). University of Central Florida's 2018 Mobile Survey Report showed overall a desire for their instructors to increase mobile learning opportunities, but the top rea-son students did not want their instructors to use apps and devices is because of limited internet connectivity on and off campus (Seilhamer et al., 2018).

Tending to ethical considerations of hardware access consists of two main considerations: reliability of the devices students have and their internet access. These are a few recommendations for being mindful of student hardware access:

1. Identify course material and activities that are bandwidth heavy, such as videos and simulations. If videos are key, share a transcript and option to download videos for offline viewing. Creating shorter videos allows more flexibility and mobile access.
2. Identify offline options in mobile learning apps and make these clear for students. If students are using a reading app like Kindle for their texts, remind students that they can read these offline.
3. Include in the syllabus and mention throughout the semester ways students can access laptops, mobile devices, webcams, and other technology they may need. Making students aware of multiple computer labs on campus is helpful, but it is even more helpful if students have the option of taking the tech wherever they need it. Such technology loans may be available through the library, student technology center, residence hall, or other offices on campus.
4. When facilitating live online sessions, make cameras optional. Turning off the camera can help lower the amount of bandwidth students need to participate in the session, or they may be on a device without a camera.
5. Continue to make print options available, with guidance on how to print out materials on campus or local options to explore (e.g., public libraries and stores with printing options).
6. If class activities require devices or Wi-Fi access, have an alternative option when the Wi-Fi acts up, student devices are not cooperating, or when students do not have devices.

Privacy and Data Sharing

Privacy and data sharing concerns exist with all technologies. Surveillance capitalism is the practice of tracking and storing user activity for profit. The issue is even greater with phones as they can track our movement along with every click and post. As marginalized populations rely on their phones more than others, they are also the most vulnerable to ed tech's ethical shortcomings from digital redlining (Gilliard, 2017) to other forms of algorithm-driven suppression or oppression (Benjamin, 2019; O'Neil, 2017). Social media is a whole other level of privacy concern: The vast majority of cases of online harassment occur on social media (Vogels, 2021). While apps collect tons of user data, we can select apps that minimize data collecting and sharing, share ways students can minimize data sharing and protect their privacy, and help students create an intentional public presence or keep personally identifiable information off of the internet. Since most if not all of our students have phones, these issues are already affecting their everyday lives, so they will greatly benefit from educational opportunities to be more mindful of their mobile tech use and online presence.

These are a few recommendations for being mindful of student privacy and data sharing:

- *Address privacy considerations in the syllabus.* Scholars concerned about student privacy in educational technology wrote a syllabus statement for any instructor to use and adapt (Caines & Glass, 2019). It provides questions for students to consider as they use technology, opening the conversation to students without requiring comprehensive Terms of Use for every technology. If you are using products not supported by your campus, ask your academic technologist about any ethical concerns regarding the app and what apps they would recommend accordingly.
- *Direct students to check the settings of their apps* for information collected and shared and change their settings accordingly.
- *Do not require students to use public-facing social media in a way that requires their name and photo.* If students are uncomfortable creating a public online presence that can be linked to them specifically, suggest that students use avatar photos or other profile photos.
- *If course activities call for it, have students use their own data for analysis.* Faculty have done this to teach quantitative research methods (Colin et al., 2021) and engage in rhetorical analysis (Vie, 2016). Having students use their own data makes the learning relevant to students' lives and teaches them firsthand how much data phones collect on and about us. For more ideas, see Students Digging Into Their Own Data in chapter 11: Teaching and Learning Activities.

Whether students take a critical pause at information collected on their whereabouts or are unperturbed by their data being collected, the point is to give students agency by making them aware of these practices and giving them options accordingly.

Attention: Pings and Other Distractions

When we use phones for course learning, we are potentially crowding students' phone screens with more push notifications. Institutions might like the idea that they can text students instead of emailing them, but unchecked such logic could result in students receiving dozens of phone notifications daily from their professors, advisors, student organizations, and other areas of the institution. Similarly, using mobile-friendly class communication spaces such as messaging apps or group platforms can result in "potentially ubiquitous and non-stop engagement" (Dennen & Hao, 2014, p. 407). If we neglect to mindfully pick such class communication methods, it can be tedious for students to figure out which messages they must pay attention to and which ones are optional.

While college students may overall favor timely and relevant reminders from institutions, as suggested by UCF's multiyear study (Seilhamer et al., 2018) and José Bowen's work and research (Stachowiak, 2019), it is important that students remain in control of notifications and that they are given ample education and opportunity to opt out of these communication. That being said, instructors should start with a default notification structure, then ask for student input and make adjustments while allowing students to set their preferences. As instructors and other educators such as instructional designers, you have a lot of perspective on what helps students succeed in their courses and how courses fit into certain academic, professional, and life paths. Your informed recommendations are going to matter, and students will likely value them too. That is why people like Bowen say that there is merit in being the main architect of how technologies work in your courses, including their mobile components.

These are a few recommendations for being mindful of notifications and other draws of student attention:

- *Talk with students about defaults notification settings:* How many messages is the right amount? What kinds of reminders are helpful, and when? Do they want reminders for every assignment due date? If so, how long before the due date? What is the default time for due dates?
- *For settings that are entirely in students' control, give them recommendations on notifications to set.* If your course has a social media component, recommend notifications for select interactions since these apps' default setting will be to notify users about everything. You might even recommend making notifications silent or in some other format that is less intrusive.
- *If you use a group messaging or communication space (e.g., Slack, Discord, GroupMe, Microsoft Teams), have students adjust their notifications and other settings as soon as they download and begin using the app.* Show them click by click how to do this in class, and also link students to instructions from the program's website. If students are overwhelmed with notifications and cannot distinguish necessary from unnecessary messages, this could be worse than getting no notifications at all.

- *Require students to receive notifications for messages from you, but offer options on how they receive those notifications.* An LMS normally does this through a discussion forum specific to announcements. In a platform like Slack or Discord, this might be a channel specific to announcements. If students do not want any notifications on their phones, ensure they can get them as an email so that they don't miss important announcements.
- *Gather ongoing feedback from students.* After a few weeks, ask students about the reminder, notification, and other communication components of their mobile apps and emails. What has been helpful, and what has been distracting? What tweaks, if any, would strike a better balance?

In support of mindful "nudges," José Bowen asked, "How can we use knowledge of human behavior to help students do more of the work only they can do?" (Stachowiak, 2019). In other words, how can we use notifications and reminders to get students to focus on the work of learning rather than keeping straight the many different logistics of four or five classes? Following the rationale in the executive function section of chapter 4: Organizing and Planning Mobile Learning, we can use a phone's behaviorist components to our benefit when we use them intentionally. The key to mobile-mindful learning is finding a balance of eliminating unwanted phone behavior and increasing helpful phone behavior.

Digital Accessibility

Digital accessibility, or web accessibility, refers to web design standards that ensure people of varying abilities can use digital content. The web content accessibility guidelines (WCAG) are commonly consulted to determine whether a website or app is accessible. In the United States around 2017, many higher education institutions received complaints or were sued for websites not complying with the Americans With Disabilities Act (ADA) and Section 508 of the Rehabilitation Act. This movement largely increased awareness and effort to make websites other digital content more accessible. The WCAGs fall into four categories: perceivable (elements can be navigated and distinguished), operable (one can control how they move through the content and use all available functions), understandable (web content is not confusing), and robust (can be used on multiple devices). In introducing digital accessibility to instructors in concrete terms of what will likely affect their instructional practices, I point to six areas:

- text appearance
- descriptive hyperlinks

- color contrast
- heading styles and other sequencing elements
- images
- captions and transcripts

More on these six areas and digital accessibility practices can be found in the Assessing Our Digital Accessibility Practices checklist in chapter 10: Course Planning Activities.

So what does this mean for mobile-mindful teaching? The WCAGs also include accessibility on mobile devices, and the W3 Initiative's most recent versions focused on updates related to mobile accessibility. This means that mobile apps are likely being designed mindful of accessibility, but that does not guarantee every app or every webpage viewed on a phone will meet accessibility guidelines. Therefore, let's start with a few accessibility considerations:

- *Implement digital accessibility practices when creating documents and text pages*, which make these pages easier to navigate on all devices.
- *Choose video and audio content with captions and transcripts.* For audio-visual content that you create, use programs available at your institution to auto-transcribe as much as possible, and then update as needed. Captions are commonly used, but especially on phones when people are in an environment where they cannot play sound.
- *Add text descriptions, or alt text, to visual media like photos and GIFs.* Doing so not only helps blind and low-vision users but also users whose devices cannot load images. Text descriptions are particularly important on social media, which tends to rely greatly on visual content. Most LMS will have a text box when adding an image to include alt text. You may be able to double-click or right-click an image to get to that area.
- *If an app version of course content is available, encourage students to use the app, which may be more usable.*

Partner With Tech Experts

I wouldn't go as far as invoking the Zelda quote, "It's dangerous to go alone!" but adding mobile-mindful learning options should not be something you have to do on your own. Use the resources you may have on your campus, whether they are instructional designers, academic technologists, faculty developers, colleagues, or others who know the technology and pedagogy to support you. Even if you are not sure what questions you have or how these professionals could help you, meet with them to share your goals and ideas and see if they have suggestions or connections to resources. Such an action not only helps you, but it also potentially helps your students. Technologists may tell you that they can visit your class to help students get their phones set for mobile-mindful learning in your course and beyond. They may lead you to options for students to access technology equipment. They may be able to explain which programs and apps rate well when it comes to privacy and usability, and potential alternatives.

If such support is limited, ask in-person and online networks of faculty and other educators about their experiences with including mobile-friendly options for course engagement. Faculty learning communities can be low-resource ways to work as a group to increase mobile-mindful options: Ask colleagues if they want to read through this book or specific mobile-mindful learning materials to explore and experiment together. Testing feedback forms you want to use in class, materials with QR codes, or the ease with which faculty can navigate your practice LMS course can help you work out issues before you offer these experiences to students.

Avoid the Tech Tax on Student Workload

With all of the doors mobile learning opens, it is tempting for our geeky selves to slip in more work for students on top of their existing workload, what has been called the "Course-and-a-Half Syndrome" in blended teaching (Stachowiak, 2016). Instead, the focus of mobile learning should be on making the current workload more accessible and manageable. As you implement new mobile learning opportunities, check for whether the workload has remained the same by comparing the new learning material and assignments to your previous design. Tools like Wake Forest University's Course Workload Estimator (Barre et al., n.d.) help communicate transparency about the learning expectations. If you use mobile-friendly content to provide students with optional reinforcement and review (a good UDL practice), clearly state what is optional versus required.

References

Barre, B., Brown, A., & Esarey, J. (n.d.). *Workload estimator 2.0*. Center for the Advancement of Teaching at Wake Forest University. https://cat.wfu.edu/resources/tools/estimator2/

Benjamin, R. (2019). *Race after technology: Abolitionist tools for the New Jim Code*. Polity.

Caines, A., & Glass, E. R. (2019, October 14). Education before regulation: Empowering students to question their data privacy. *EDUCAUSE*. https://er.educause.edu/articles/2019/10/education-before-regulation-empowering-students-to-question-their-data-privacy

Colin, M., Eastman, S., Merrill, M., & Rockey, A. (2021, March 19). Leveraging mobile technology to achieve teaching goals. *EDUCAUSE Review.* https://er.educause.edu/articles/2021/3/leveraging-mobile-technology-to-achieve-teaching-goals

Dennen, V., & Hao, S. (2014). Intentionally mobile pedagogy: The M-COPE framework for mobile learning in higher education. *Technology, Pedagogy, and Education, 23*(3), 397–419. https://doi.org/10.1080/1475939X.2014.943278

Galanek, J. D., Gierdowski, D. C., & Brooks, D. C. (2018, October). *ECAR study of undergraduate students and information technology, 2018.* https://www.educause.edu/ecar/research-publications/ecar-study-of-undergraduate-students-and-information-technology/2018/device-use-and-importance

Gilliard, C. (2017, July 3). Pedagogy and the logic of platforms. *EDUCAUSE.* https://er.educause.edu/articles/2017/7/pedagogy-and-the-logic-of-platforms

Lang, J. (2020). *Distracted: Why students can't focus and what you can do about it.* Basic Books.

O'Neil, C. (2017). *Weapons of math destruction: How Big Data increases inequality and threatens democracy.* Crown.

Perrin, A. (2021, June 3). *Mobile technology and home broadband 2021.* Pew Research Center. https://www.pewresearch.org/internet/2021/06/03/mobile-technology-and-home-broadband-2021/

Pew Research Center. (2019, November 20). *Mobile divides in emerging economies.* https://www.pewresearch.org/internet/2019/11/20/mobile-divides-in-emerging-economies/

Pew Research Center. (2021, April 17). *Mobile facts sheet (2021).* https://www.pewresearch.org/internet/fact-sheet/mobile/

Seilhamer, R., Chen, B., deNoyelles, A., Raible, J., Bauer, J., & Salter, A. (2018). *2018 mobile survey report.* UCF Center for Distributed Learning: University of Central Florida. https://digitallearning.ucf.edu/msi/research/mobile/survey2018/

Selfe, C. L. (1999). Technology and literacy: A story about the perils of not paying attention. *College Composition and Communication, 50*(3), 411–436. https://doi.org/10.2307/358859

Stachowiak, B. (Host). (2016, August 11). Blended course design (No. 113) [Audio podcast episode]. In *Teaching in higher ed.* https://teachinginhighered.com/podcast/blended-course-design

Stachowiak, B. (Host). (2019, April 18). Spaces, places (and nudges) (No. 253) [Audio podcast episode]. In *Teaching in higher ed.* https://teachinginhighered.com/podcast/spaces-and-places-and-nudges/

Vie, S. (2016). Critical literacies in mobile social games: Terms of service, privacy policies, and game analysis. In C. Lutkewitte (Ed.), *Mobile technologies and the writing classroom: Resources for teachers* (pp. 82–98). National Council of Teachers of English.

Vogels, E. (2021, February 16). *Online harassment occurs most often on social media, but strikes in other places, too*. Pew Research Center. https://www.pewresearch.org/fact-tank/2021/02/16/online-harassment-occurs-most-often-on-social-media-but-strikes-in-other-places-too/

Walker, A. (2019, November 19). *Americans favor mobile devices over desktops and laptops for getting news*. Pew Research Center. https://www.pewresearch.org/fact-tank/2019/11/19/americans-favor-mobile-devices-over-desktops-and-laptops-for-getting-news/

6

PREPARE STUDENTS FOR MOBILE LEARNING

E ven though many college students may not be able to remember a time before smartphones, this familiarity does not mean students are accustomed to using their phones for formal learning. Furthermore, they "have been exposed to the idea that smartphones are hazardous to one's cognitive health" (Miller, 2022, pp. 173–174). Students receive cues from their teachers that their digital literacy practices are incompatible with "real" learning and, therefore, perceive their digital learning as inferior to more traditional forms (Cohn, 2016). Such cues have been around since the increase of personal computers in education, when instructors believed "the students with whom we work are made of much finer stuff than the machine in our midst" (Selfe, 1999, p. 414). For "the kind of cultural strangeness" (p. 413) we might struggle with when it comes to increasing mobile learning opportunities, "we can no longer deny that we live in a society that increasingly requires students to participate in civic action through digital portals, regardless of their age, exposure, or experience with these devices" (Cohn, 2021, p. 19).

Because students are used to messages about the perils of learning with phones, make new mobile learning opportunities explicit to them. Their familiarity with phones can still come in handy: For example, students may be familiar with how to take a screenshot, but if they have only taken them for social media purposes rather than note-taking or data collection, they may need to plan and work through how to best save those screenshots. Fortunately, there is reason to believe many students will embrace these options. According to 2019 Pew Research survey data, teenagers identified three main reasons they are on their phones: to pass the time (90%), connect with others (84%), and learn new things (83%). Students are mobile learners, and they could be for your class if the material were available and they knew how to best use it. College students want more opportunities to use their phones for course learning (Gierdowski, 2019).

As with any pedagogical change we have made, we want to make sure the change benefits student learning the way we intend. Understandably, we can be discouraged when students do not seem to notice these changes or benefit from them. It is often not that the change is not beneficial, but that students have to be our partners in making the change happen. If students are used to course formats that are strictly designed for offline and desktop-based learning, students may not even recognize that your pedagogy has opened up learning possibilities on their phones. Be explicit with how students can be mobile learners, and get their input on ways to increase mobile learning.

Because mindfully including mobile learning options may be new for you and for students, invite their feedback throughout the semester. Gathering this feedback does not have to be labor intensive: If you survey students early in the semester to get to know their learning strengths, preferences, resources, and needs, add both questions and answer options that account for mobile learning. In the Required and Recommended Materials section of the syllabus, list mobile apps you recommend students download and use (this and more suggestions are included in the Mobile-Mindful Syllabus section of chapter 10: Course Planning Activities). If your institution's LMS has a mobile app, direct students to use it for specific purposes, such as receiving reminders and checking due dates and grades. As you discuss reading assignments and other activities, explain how students can access these on their phones. In addition to the ways you have planned for mobile learning options, ask students about how they use their phones for school: Have they read textbooks or completed assignments on their phones? Do they use phones for their courses out of necessity or because phones provide specific learning benefits? Do they find these strategies useful, or is it a struggle to complete activities on a phone? Studies have established that students are using their phones for coursework, but these studies have not always explored students' experiences learning with phones. Asking the students in front of us what works well and what presents barriers can help us prioritize our mobile-mindful approaches.

Because we are approaching mobile-mindful learning as an additional option among fluid learning options, students do not need to feel that they will be forced to do their coursework on phones. Furthermore, you may also not feel all coursework should be done from a phone. Therefore, make your recommendations clear for which technologies may be most conducive to specific activities. For activities that require complex conceptualization, you might suggest students do this work with handwriting or a large screen that allows for conceptual maps while also suggesting students take photos of their handwritten maps and save them to a class photo album. For group projects, suggest students plan communication methods that work well across all devices, so that students can not only stay in touch via phone but also attach files or refer to work more extensively when they are in front of a laptop. For live class sessions that take place online, recommend students use a computer that allows them to better see the shared screen and participate in chat. Also direct students to use the web conferencing app on their phone if no other option is available and provide recommendations on how to best participate. If you notice at least one student somewhat regularly attends a class session from a phone, be aware that it is more difficult for them to see the chat window, and relay any comments or questions they may not be able to see.

Do not be discouraged if it takes time for you and students to fit mobile learning into the flow of course activities: Implementing a new technology tends to feel awkward even if you are well-prepared. We might recall a time when we found it awkward to read journal articles on a computer rather than print and transfer our digital reading notes to a document rather than write them in a notebook. With frequency, that process likely got smoother, enough that we could enjoy the efficiency that comes with adding digital strategies. The same will come with mobile learning if we allow plenty of time for practice.

SUGGESTED ACTIVITY: TASK MANAGEMENT AND REGULATION VIA MOBILE

Younger students new to college may be learning how to plan academic work for multiple courses, each instructor using different ways to organize their course, scaffold learning, and communicate with students. Additionally, students may be used to separating phone use from productivity. Have a class discussion about how students organize their lives and tasks, and how they use their phones to support this management. Offer a model as a starting point: Since most people are familiar with and have access to Google products, Google Calendar is a powerful example of many management features such as Events, Tasks, and Reminders.

Since class meeting times are limited, a weekly discussion forum could promote this kind of core skill development in a way that allows students to get to know one another. See an example of what I call "Class Citizenship Behaviors," based on organizational citizenship behaviors (Moore, 2016), which prompts students once a week to share tips and resources with one another on how to best do their work as students. Students might share screenshots of apps they like to use to stay organized, or realize that they could use a new way of organizing their tasks.

Wherever you list course text assignments and activities, include in the title the time you estimate it will take to do that activity. An easy first step may be with readings, videos, audio, and other texts, as some of these come with durations already and others can be estimated. For text reading, start with estimating 200 words per minute, and then tweak depending on density and intended application of the reading material. Adding the estimated time in the link name itself helps students determine whether they have the appropriate amount of time to dedicate to the activity at that moment, and it helps them plan for when they will do each activity.

Example:

- The Little Problem I Had Renting a House (video: 14 minutes, TED Talk)
- How Fear Took Over the American Suburbs (article: 7-minute read)
- The Red Line: Racial Disparities in Lending (podcast episode: 52 minutes with transcript)

With a list like this, a student can download the podcast episode for offline listening, listen to the podcast episode during their 20-minute commute (40 minutes round trip), and use their walk across campus to employ the "podcast pause" and take notes on what they have listened to so far. They might watch the video when they can connect to wireless internet and save the article for whenever they have a spare 10 minutes, making sure they save the link somewhere they will be able to access quickly and easily. I began implementing this practice in the LMS long before I started thinking about mobile learning. The practice is particularly helpful for students planning out their learning across time and place, allowing more time to think and reflect between activities rather than barreling through every activity at once. This estimated time practice also promotes Mary-Ann Winkelmes' (2014) transparency in learning and teaching (TILT) framework, a way to make tacit learning expectations clearer to students. For a deeper evaluation of estimated time related to coursework, such as time per week spent on the course or how long it will take a student to write a paper, see the Workload Estimator from the Center for the Advancement of Teaching at Wake Forest University (Barre et al., n.d.).

References

Barre, B., Brown, A., & Esarey, J. (n.d.). *Workload Estimator 2.0.* Center for the Advancement of Teaching at Wake Forest University. https://cat.wfu.edu/resources/tools/estimator2/

Cohn, J. (2016). "Devilish smartphones" and the "stone-cold" Internet: Implications of the technology addiction trope in college student digital literacy narratives. *Computers and Composition, 42,* 80–94. https://doi.org/10.1016/j.compcom.2016.08.008

Cohn, J. (2021). *Skim, dive, surface: Teaching digital reading.* West Virginia University Press.

Gierdowski, D. C. (2019, October). *ECAR study of undergraduate students and information technology, 2019.* https://library.educause.edu/resources/2019/10/2019-study-of-undergraduate-students-and-information-technology

Miller, M. D. (2022). *Remembering and forgetting in the age of technology: Teaching, learning, and the science of memory in a wired world.* West Virginia Press.

Moore, C. (2016, May/June). The future of work: What Google shows us about the present and future of online collaboration. *TechTrends, 60*(3), 233–244. https://doi.org/10.1007/s11528-016-0044-5

Pew Research Center. (2019, November 20). *Mobile divides in emerging economies.* www.pewresearch.org/internet/2019/11/20/mobile-divides-in-emerging-economies/

Selfe, C. L. (1999). Technology and literacy: A story about the perils of not paying attention. *College Composition and Communication, 50*(3), 411–436. https://doi.org/10.2307/358859

Winkelmes, M. (2014). *TILT higher ed: Transparency in learning and teaching.* https://tilthighered.com/

7

SOCIAL LEARNING AS A MOBILE-MINDFUL CLASS

While social learning is valued in theory, our educational systems and practices favor individual performance. Because the time classmates spend together in the same place and time is limited at best, we can use social technologies to help keep the class connected and learning from one another. With "[a] social take on learning, [we acknowledge] that meaningful and transformational learning usually comes unexpectedly, while working and interacting with others." To create opportunities for this transformational learning, we need to "create and multiply the appropriate contexts and containers for informal learning to happen" (Centre for Community Organizations, 2019, p. 42). Creating online social places easily accessible on a phone is crucial to allowing the type of community and longevity that allows impactful learning (Moore, 2021).

Class meetings should not be the only "contexts and containers" for students to learn from one another, as these comprise a small share of time related to the course and can be difficult to engage all students. Spaces for social learning could include social media spaces (e.g., Facebook Groups, Twitter hashtags) or more private, comprehensive community spaces like Slack, Microsoft Teams, and Discord. The following is an example of what such a social learning environment could look like.

Hypothetical Example: Mobile-Mindful Social Learning

When a student is taking a "podcast pause" while listening to a 52-minute episode on racial disparities in lending, she thinks of a related personal story. She remembers you encouraged the class to "check in" with their learning during the week, so in a couple of taps she gets to a class Slack channel. Since she is walking, she uses voice-to-text to capture this:

> Just listened to how hard of a time a single Black woman had getting approved for a mortgage. The lender told her it was because she was a contract worker, but her white friend who was in a similar line of work and had a similar credit score got approved with far fewer hoops to jump through. The crazy hoops one has to jump through reminded me of my cousin who had a crazy difficult time getting a mortgage for a condo. While she had been employed full time at a great job in the auto industry for almost 10 years, they kept scrutinizing every aspect of her finances. I had never heard of anything like that. Now I'm thinking, were her finances suspicious because she was a single Latina mom?

She quickly scans the message to make sure the transcription makes sense, and hits Send. By the time she takes a seat in her next class, she sees her comment has been liked four times, and two people have responded with questions or agreeing that they've heard of similar stories. She thinks over these comments and realizes that lending officers have the discretion to make people jump through these hoops, but they increase these hoops for those they are skeptical of and biased toward, and it makes her think of how many other areas of life this affects.

How to Facilitate Mobile-Mindful Social Learning

This hypothetical example of social, ubiquitous learning shows how much learning can be extended by being able to share an idea with a group from wherever you are learning and receive feedback right away. Group spaces like Slack, Discord, and Microsoft Teams are increasingly being used as communication spaces for courses because they allow immediacy, reactions (e.g., thumbs up, likes, emojis), and more ways to express one's self and respond to one another. When students experience reciprocity, whether in reactions or other types of responses, they are likely to be motivated to continue posting and sharing. Even those who are more passive in such spaces still have more opportunities to hear about course concepts through their classmates' ideas and experiences.

This type of interaction can be difficult to achieve in an LMS discussion forum, which requires more clicks to compose a message and more time in between posting, receiving, and potentially hearing a response. While there is some capability to add reactions, this is limited and not widespread. Going beyond the LMS opens the possibility of communities beyond the classroom: For example, Alvarez Vazquez et al. (2020) found that Slack provided a single communication space for a cardiovascular engineering course, bringing together students from different institutions and education levels.

While the type of sharing offered in the hypothetical example does not involve sources and citations with polished prose, the learning takes the crucial step of connecting to real-world situations and having that connection be acknowledged. In sharing stories like these in connection to course content, students get to know one another better and discover ways their lives are invested in class concepts. In such spaces, students are more likely to converse with one another on course topics more often, which will give their ideas depth when it comes time to write a more academic, comprehensive piece.

As discussed in chapter 5 regarding ethical considerations, we will want to give students plenty of upfront guidance on how to set their notification preferences to make sure students are not overwhelmed with class posting and activities. Determine what group communication platform will work best based on the course learning outcomes, activities, and campus technology (a good opportunity to partner with tech professionals on campus). Set up the collaborative space(s) accordingly, and then get input from students. Should students be allowed to create their own subchannels (basically threads for specific topics or people), or should they have to request a channel from the professor? What is the etiquette surrounding how late or early in the day students post? Other netiquette discussions should apply, such as ground rules for civil discourse and how to handle harassing and discriminatory behaviors. Also consider the preferences of people at ends of the spectrum, from the student who wants as few notifications and interactions as possible to the student who is posting constantly. Such discussion and consideration should help ensure the likely scenario that students will not only get a lot out of the space but also feel they can come to you if something is not working.

These examples of making the class social on mobile take place in a private space dedicated to a class, maybe inviting the occasional class visitor or other student group to join. There are added opportunities when social learning extends to more public spaces such as blogs and social media.

Opening the Door to Social Media for Teaching and Learning

After considering how to add social media to your learning ecologies, let's now consider what opportunities social media could provide for teaching and learning. I propose "opening the door" rather than rushing through it. Using the UDL framework, you could first consider how students can use social media to identify examples of course concepts or otherwise demonstrate their learning and disseminate their ideas. You can test social media's possibilities, not only seeing what unique contributions social media adds to student learning and expression but also where students could boost their social media literacy in order to achieve learning outcomes. For example, if you see a student has used Twitter to ask for recommendations related to the course, discover and retweet scholars they follow on Twitter, and later cite these scholars in their coursework, such frequent activity can provide a powerful comparison to other ways students express their learning. More than imagining social media's potential, you can see samples of social media-enabled learning and use such work to provide future students with examples and guidelines.

Depending on your discipline and course learning outcomes, you may eventually move toward a learning activity that gets everyone on social media. If you require or strongly recommend your students participate on a social media platform, ensure students have the support to do so in a way that is safe and effective. See the recommendations for social media in chapter 10: Course Planning Activities.

As Always, Know Thy Students

It is easy to make assumptions about social media use, especially when it comes to younger adults. The longer one pays attention to how students learn with technology, the clearer it becomes that while younger college students have always been around technology, this does not necessarily mean students have learned to use it strategically, professionally, and to its full potential. Even if most of your students have one social media account, they may use it infrequently or have negative perceptions of social media, which may come out of messages they have received about anything related to their smartphones (Cohn, 2016). They may also have pressing safety and privacy concerns and past instances of harassment.

Before integrating social media into the course, ask students about their use and perceptions of social media. This could be an anonymous survey asking students what social media platforms they use, how often they use them, and what types of course content or learning activities they would like to be available through social media. This anonymous glance at your class paired with conversation on the topic may help you know whether it is most effective to share 45-second intro-to-the-week videos on TikTok or create a Facebook group for the class.

Exploring Existing Content

If you have added social media to your learning ecology as suggested in chapter 3, you may already be exploring existing social media content. Now you might consider how existing social media content could enrich your courses and benefit students. As you browse social media, save content that relates directly to your courses either through an in-app curation tool such as Twitter Bookmarks and Facebook's Saved Posts, taking screenshots and saving them to a specific folder (if the content is public, which is indicated in the poster's name line), or saving links to original content in another location. Then tap into these examples in class.

Students can also be prompted to explore social media content themselves. You can suggest a list of accounts to follow and have students evaluate their content or explore other accounts that could be added to your list. Social media content is a powerful source of data for empirical research, so if your course includes research skills and opportunities, invite students to explore data readily available to the public on social media. The Teaching and Learning Activities in chapter 11 include one example of how students can use social media for research.

Sharing Teacher Content

If your curiosity is piqued about developing your teaching presence on social media, you could use whatever platform works best for you and your students to share reminders, demonstrations, quizzes (for recall rather than assessment), feedback, polls, and discussion questions. Pay attention to what other educators are doing on one or two platforms, noting their teaching strategies, interactions, frequency, and other factors.

Social media platforms are increasingly visual, so using eye-catching media will work better than text alone. Short-and-sweet video is likely most effective, as moving content best draws attention. Content-specific funny images and memes can provide helpful, relatable ways for students to learn course concepts. Plus, as students have limited face time with their instructors, video adds teaching presence and an opportunity to communicate and reinforce expertise and care.

For your sanity, keep it fluid and plan it out. If you think social media would be useful for reminders and demonstrations, plan these in advance and perhaps create the content all at once. For example, you could plan out reminders of important dates such as project due dates and campus events. You may also decide to reshare a key video or illustration at strategic points in the semester to encourage repetition and practice. Reminders that stay constant, such as visiting the writing center a week before a paper due date or to meet with you during office hours, can be a series of 30-second recordings that you can post when the right time in the semester comes. (If you include dates, do this with text features on the app and keep the video content itself general.)

Similarly, you may be able to identify three occasions to demonstrate something you do at least once a term and for which students often need extra support and reinforcement, such as how to properly apply a tourniquet, use different pronouns based on context in a different language, and identify examples of different ergonomic designs. A short video that can be shared on social media—maybe even multiple times throughout the semester—can help increase the frequency with which the student sees, hears, and thinks through the action.

In addition to preplanned content, embrace the timeliness and spontaneity of social media. Analyze something you see on social media through your expert lens by quote tweeting (retweeting with a comment) an example of a class concept with a hashtag for the course, using screenshots to record a video response on TikTok, or annotating a photo on Instagram. When you see a course concept "in the wild," capture a photo or video and post it on the spot. While this content is less polished, it communicates to students that the stuff they are learning *right now* is working in the world around them.

Keep it fluid, and plan for a design that works even if current students don't actively follow you. Your social media activity might be useful for students, but it could also be used to curate instructional material you may implement in courses or refer to during lectures and discussions. The video you recorded analyzing a photo you took may be a good asynchronous online activity in which students are first invited to analyze a photo related to course concepts and then you provide your video analysis.

Since many courses involve some form of peer review and providing feedback, social media is also a great opportunity to model feedback. Students can see you responding to people's posts, statements from texts, and other material within or beyond class. You can demonstrate feedback and then during class explain the strategies you use in the feedback. Beyond modeling, it can also be a way to give feedback and show students your enthusiasm and attention to students' ideas.

Audience Is Complicated on Social Media

Often referred to as "context collapse" (Marwick & boyd, 2011), publicly available social media content means that your audience may not be whom you anticipate. Even though you may post content with your students in mind, you may have students in other classes or other institutions engaging with your content, or other instructors and educators. When I asked a colleague about her audience on her professor-themed TikTok account, she explained that out of her 11,000+ followers, only a few were her actual students, at least that she knew of (VaNessa Thompson, personal communication, February 16, 2022). Her content is a mix of generalizable advice and experience for anyone in higher education and specific references to her course concepts and institution.

While you can't always control your audience, you do not necessarily have to cater to every audience. You can still choose to post with your immediate student audience in mind, or perhaps colleagues who teach similar subjects, but expect the unexpected when it comes to who may interact with you. As you may explain to students, you can always limit certain interactions and make your account more private, but it helps to act with the assumption that your content can be seen by anyone.

Avoid Sharing Identifiable Student Content Without Permission

It is not uncommon for faculty to share samples of student work or communication on Twitter, for well- and ill-intentioned reasons. Before any other logistical discussion here, choose care and consideration when it comes to students. If you are going to social media to troubleshoot a challenging situation with a student, keep it generalizable with the goal in mind of keeping the action as constructive as possible. If you are referring to student work or comments in a public platform, remove identifiable information or get clear permission from students to do so.

References

Alvarez Vazquez, E., Cortes-Mendez, M., Striker, R., Singelmann, L., Pearson, M., & Swartz, E. M. (2020, June). Lessons learned using Slack in engineering education: An innovation-based learning approach. *2020 ASEE Virtual Annual Conference Content Access.* https://doi.org/10.18260/1-2--34916

Centre for Community Organizations. (2019). *White supremacy culture in organizations.* Coco-net.org

Cohn, J. (2016). "Devilish smartphones" and the "stone-cold" Internet: Implications of the technology addiction trope in college student digital literacy narratives. *Computers and Composition, 42,* 80–94. https://doi.org/10.1016/j.compcom.2016.08.008

Marwick, A. E., & boyd, d. (2011). I tweet honestly, I tweet passionately: Twitter users, context collapse, and the imagined audience. *New Media & Society, 13,* 114–133. https://doi.org/10.1177/1461444810365313

Moore, C. M. (2021). *How faculty use online social spaces to develop their teaching practices: An ethnographic study of the #ungrading online community* [Dissertation, Oakland University]. ProQuest Dissertations Publishing.

8

DIVE INTO MOBILE-FIRST OPPORTUNITIES

After evaluating your current instructional materials and making tweaks to increase mobile access, identify learning activities that are particularly conducive to mobile learning. In chapters 2–4 on learning how to be mobile-mindful, some mobile learning approaches may have resonated with you and sparked ideas for how your students could benefit from them. If storytelling and lecture are integral instructional moves, you may want to explore more audio options. If demonstrations are the main mode of instruction and assessment, you may want to lean into video demonstrations, which are flexible across devices, time, and context. If your course requires students to draw from a vast knowledge base, creating flashcards collaboratively and other frequent retrieval opportunities could be a game changer. If mobile options provide a huge learning boost to your students, try a mobile-first approach to these activities, which means content is designed with mobile in mind but is also available in other modes. Let's consider a few possibilities related to learning modes previously discussed.

Mobile-First Reading

When students become comfortable with doing some course readings on their phones, annotating those readings, recording ideas for a project wherever they come up, and saving articles they come across in their phone scrolling, they will have a wealth of notes and foundational thinking at their disposal when it is time to sit in front of a laptop for an hour to begin writing an academic paper.

- *Favor longer texts available in e-reader formats, then offer additional options from there.* In doing so, identify a few support pages or help docs from the publisher that will help students learn how to use useful reading tools, such as annotating the text and exporting those notes in a way that students can use. Then explain how these notes will apply to the course, such as quotes they should be ready to use to support a point in class discussion or in writing.

- *Explain your recommended practices for reading e-texts.* Similar to how reading discussions may involve students pouring over their print books, you could project the cloud reader on a screen, search for quotations students provide, and show students how to highlight, annotate, and save notes. This process could be a way for you to curate and export notes based on the collective discussion while modeling digital active reading strategies.
- *Favor short, granular readings.* Select shorter articles, even if it means offering more of them.
- *Take advantage of open access materials,* which give you freedom to remix and redistribute the content. If the open access material isn't mobile-accessible, you could divide it into shorter chunks and put it in a format that scales well on a phone.
- *If journal articles are among your course texts, link students to the library's article page rather than the PDF or offer both links.* Journal article pages often offer the content in multiple formats such as plain text or audio.

The Travel Narratives in Literature case study in chapter 9 offers related examples and ideas for navigating reading format choices.

As you level up your digital and mobile reading game, you might also take advantage of social annotation apps like Perusall and Hypothesis, which both are compatible with mobile devices and offer LMS integrations. The following QR code (see Figure 8.1) will not only take you to an article explaining how

Figure 8.1. QR code to access "How to Use Hypothesis on Mobile Devices."

to use Hypothesis on a mobile device ("How to Use Hypothesis on Mobile Devices," n.d.), but it will also show you the annotations others have made on the article. Browse how the reading and annotation works on a phone, as public annotations can be viewed without an account.

Mobile-First Audio and Visual

Multimedia materials offer great options if your teaching strengths include storytelling, lecturing, and interviews with guest speakers. Such resources can be used from course to course.

- *Include texts that offer an audio reading option.* Ask publishers what audio options are available for their texts and make students aware of these options. Since journal article pages sometimes offer an audio version, link students to the article landing page. Increasingly, PDF reading programs and word processing programs (e.g., Microsoft Word) offer "read aloud" options.

- *Make audio and video playlists part of "required reading,"* shared both in a neutral format of a doc with links to source material and as a playlist within an audio or video app. Choose content with captions and transcripts. Apply similar principles for creating photo albums and ensuring accessibility with text descriptions.

- *Consider enhancing or extending the availability of a live lecture, case study, guest speaker interview, or demonstration by offering an additional recorded audio or video option.* You might choose one of these because it is integral to the course. It may be something referred to or reviewed multiple times in the course. It may be content you use in multiple sections of a course and in other contexts. Perhaps it is long and therefore not the best use of live class time, or its resulting discussion is among the longest and most robust. If the content allows for it, you could record the video content in such a way that students can watch the video or just listen to the audio.

- *Explore and enhance other multimodal formats*: instead of a video, create narrated PowerPoints that can be exported as mp3s (see an example in the chapter 9 Case Study: Fundamentals of Professional Nursing Practice). For a truly mobile-first approach, explore slides made for a phone screen such as templates on Canva. Microlearning platforms such as 7taps offer such slides with the option to add audio and visual content.

- *Offer students the option to create audio and visual presentations rather than an in-class presentation.* Then, have presenters facilitate a discussion or

Q & A in an online space (LMS discussion forum, social media group, communication channel).

- *Partner with an instructional designer or academic technologist* to guide you through creating audio and visual content including the tools to use and the process for recording, editing, producing captions and a transcript, and publishing. Their expertise will be needed especially if you want to add interactive content such as hotspots (items viewers can click within a video) and quizzes. Plan with them how this guidance and more support can be offered to students producing multimodal projects.

- *If you want to develop rich, ongoing audio or visual content through lectures, interviews, and student contributions, take workshops or courses on starting a podcast or creating instructional videos.* Many of these learning opportunities start small and simple: organizations like the Online Learning Consortium have offered 3- to 6-day workshops on these topics, and Karen Costa's (2020) book *99 Tips for Creating Simple and Sustainable Educational Videos* provides practical tips and video examples. Alpe Audio app wrote a short piece on how to write an audio course (Zlotogorski, 2020) if you want to create more intentional, interactive audio content.

See these related examples and ideas:

- Case Study: Fundamentals of Professional Nursing Practice (chapter 9)
- Course Activity: Spreading the Word on Campus With QR Codes and Multimodal Messages (chapter 11)
- Course Activity: Untether the Research Presentation (chapter 11)
- Primary Research Example: Contribute a Conversation, Gather Research With StoryCorps (chapter 11)
- Primary Research Example: Shared Photo Album (chapter 11)

Mobile-First Retrieval Practice and Memory

Designing learning material for frequent practice is one of the richest mobile-first opportunities, especially if we know our courses throw a lot at students and build on a lot of foundational knowledge.

- *Have student groups create digital flashcards in sharable decks.* You or other students can update flashcards as needed, which add to a library of flashcards for future use. Anki and Quizlet are two popular, well-established flashcard apps.

- *Send students short review activities to complete throughout the week.* There are countless ways to do this, but it should be brief and not labor intensive for the students or you. Making them ungraded and just for students to practice and keep their minds working on course content helps everyone focus on the learning rather than the grades. While Kahoot is often used to prompt students to answer questions on their phones during live class sessions, management information systems instructor Amy Rutledge posts Kahoots to the LMS so students can compete against the computer (personal communication, April 20, 2022). Additionally, a biology professor prompted students to practice identifying the vertebrate animals by the photos she posted on Snapchat (Rockey et al., 2019).
- *At the end of each class session, have students share their "one-minute papers,"* or summaries of the most important points in class, in a shared document or other shared space. After a few class sessions, have student groups turn these papers into flashcards.
- *At the beginning of a class session, have students complete a 5-minute mobile-friendly quiz to assess the concepts they learned about in reading or other course prep materials.* Have the answers show up on the screen anonymously to talk through answers and point back to texts as needed. (Bonus: Send students this quiz a few days before the class period both to assess their understanding and prompt them to prepare for class.)

Mobile-First Executive Function

We don't want students to get so caught up in the course logistics that they have little remaining bandwidth to do the actual learning of the course. Designing a course that wrangles in a smartphone's notifications powers for good will not only help students stay on task in a timely manner but also will likely give students mobile-first task management skills that will benefit their personal and professional lives. Once determining the most ethical and beneficial communication structure between you and your students as discussed in the earlier ethical considerations section in chapter 5, consider these mobile-first executive function practices.

- *Discuss how students can use the LMS mobile app* to get timely notifications about instructor announcements, upcoming due dates, and graded items. An instructional designer or academic technologist could provide this guidance or share support materials with this information.

- *Send reminders to students*, especially if there has been a change in the course schedule or other regular processes. Some of these can even be automated or scheduled.
- *Create a shared calendar for the course*, which may include due dates, class sessions, reminders, and appointment slots for student hours. Create it yourself and allow students to add it to their calendars, or have students do this early in the semester as a form of syllabus review.
- *Direct students to information on how to decrease negative mobile habits and increase positive ones*, such as the Center for Humane Technology's Take Control webpage (2021). This encouragement could make your students less distracted overall.

See Course Activity: Sending "Did You Know?" Syllabus-Based Reminders in chapter 11 for related examples and ideas.

In Review: Toward Mobile-Mindful Teaching

This section takes the leap from exploring mobile learning basics on your own to implementing mobile-mindful teaching. We have covered a lot, so let's review these recommendations to help us see the path ahead. After the review are case studies to help ground these mobile-mindful teaching moves in real course situations.

- *Start by taking a mobile test drive through your existing courses*. See which activities and materials scale well on a phone and which do not, and evaluate where small tweaks can improve mobile access. See chapter 5 for more on taking a mobile test drive.
- *Explore options for accessing the LMS*. Download the associated app to compare the usability of your LMS course pages through the mobile app versus the mobile browser.
- *Plan the flow of tech during classroom sessions*. Rather than total tech bans, consider which class activities could work well with devices and when you might encourage students to set aside the screens. For activities that intentionally invite tech use, provide QR codes and shortened URLs so that students can easily access them on their devices.
- *Keep open the offline print option*. If possible, have printouts and other ways for people without devices to participate even if others are using phones and laptops. In addition to providing another option when Wi-Fi access and devices act up, print versions allow students to keep distractions at bay.

- *Use phones and laptops to gather timely student feedback during class.* Phones are great for asking review questions, to check understanding, and to overall take the temperature of the course, all of which can help you best use your class time.
- *As you actively include mobile-mindful learning options, tend to the ethical considerations that come along with related technology* such as hardware, privacy and data sharing, attention and notifications, and accessibility. Give students guidance on how to use the technology in a way they are comfortable with, and design activities so that students can participate without a phone.
- *Partner with tech experts at your institution* who can help you plan for mobile-mindful teaching and learning, such as instructional designers and academic technologists.
- *As you make gains in adding mobile-mindful learning options, avoid the "tech tax,"* or adding to students' existing workload. Mobile-mindful options should make it easier for students to meet current course expectations.
- *Once you have planned for mobile-mindful teaching, prepare students to be mobile-mindful learners.* Make explicit what mobile learning options are available and your recommendations for getting the most out of these options.
- *Set up the right space for class communication.* If you stick with options in the LMS, encourage students to download the app so that they receive timely notifications. If you want a more organic, community-building space, explore a mobile-friendly group platform. Plan with students how this space should work, such as ways for students to appropriately communicate with you and with each other.
- *Open the door to social media, but don't force students or yourself through it.* Social media can be a rich site for connecting course content to other social contexts and people, but students may have reservations about engaging in such a public venue. Start with inviting students to explore existing content, and then consider how you can curate and engage with social media content that can then be brought into the class space.
- *As you increase mobile-mindful options, dabble in mobile-first opportunities.* If students gravitate toward certain learning actions on their phones, lean into these opportunities. When adding or planning new course material, start with how it works on a phone, and then ensure other online and offline access accordingly.

References

Center for Humane Technology. (2021). *Take control.* humanetech.com/take-control

Costa, K. (2020). *99 tips for creating simple and sustainable educational videos: A guide for online teachers and flipped classes.* Stylus.

How to use Hypothesis on mobile devices. (n.d.). *hypothes.is.* https://via.hypothes.is/ https://web.hypothes.is/help/how-to-use-hypothesis-on-mobile-devices/

Rockey, A., Eastman, S., Colin, M., & Merrill, M. (2019). Spotlighting innovative use cases of mobile learning. *The Emerging Learning Design Journal, 6*(1), 13–15. https://digitalcommons.montclair.edu/eldj/vol6/iss1/3/

Zlotogorski, Y. (2020, October 30). How to write an audio course. *Alpe Audio Blog.* https://www.alpeaudio.com/post/how-to-write-an-audio-course

MOBILE-MINDFUL ACTIVITIES

PART THREE

NOBLE-MINDFUL ACTIVITIES

9

CASE STUDIES IN MOBILE-MINDFUL TEACHING

E ven with the knowledge, recommendations, and tools at your
disposal, it can be difficult to see how it will all come together and
actually work with your students and courses. This chapter provides
concrete examples of how existing courses can add mobile-mindful options
by reviewing syllabi from different disciplines and evaluating them for
mobile-mindful teaching and learning opportunities. I read through each
syllabus (thanks to my colleagues who shared them) with the questions and
considerations outlined in the Mobile-Mindful Syllabus activity in chapter
10, and I have shared here challenges and opportunities uniquely offered by
these courses. In doing so, these analyses prioritize a few mobile-mindful
approaches rather than radically transforming every aspect of these courses.

The goal is not to arrive at mobile options for every text and learning activity, but to engage in asking questions and making inquiries about
mobile learning, acknowledging mobile limitations, and identifying promising opportunities. Each case will connect to guidelines, concepts, and
resources offered in this book. By reading through these cases, you may start
to see how you could analyze your courses for mobile learning opportunities
using the Course Planning Activities proceeding these cases.

Case Study: Travel Narratives in Literature

Carol Hart's Honors College literature course analyzes travel narratives spanning the globe over the past 3 centuries, exploring questions such as the following:

> What prejudices and preconceptions do travelers carry with them? How are they confirmed or wiped away by the worlds they encounter? How do travelers from colonizing nations regard the colonized? How do the colonized view the colonizers?

The on-campus class is a writing intensive course, for which students keep a portfolio of their work. The course assignments consist of text analyses, writing assignments, and quizzes, and the two culminating assignments are a research project and oral presentation.

Required Readings

Students must secure eight narrative books, none too voluminous. Hart could consider how students may be motivated by e-book prices and provide recommendations on how to best engage in reading for the course. For example, five of the eight required texts would be free to listen to with Audible, Amazon's audiobook program. Hart said she didn't realize students would taking advantage of these audio versions until they told her they were actively using them (personal communication, May 12, 2022). Kindle versions offer a small savings on all except two, one of which was $1 more expensive on Kindle and another that offered a $1 option on Kindle. If the class will most often use the *Cambridge Introduction to Travel Writing* in class, this may be a good one to buy in print. If other texts are shorter, link students to guides on how to get the most out of reading on Kindle or any digital reader, such as using the Cloud Reader app to read on a desktop, add annotations, and export those annotations for writing discussion forum posts and papers. (I discussed how I got the most out of reading a course text on my phone in the earlier Mobile Reading section of chapter 3.) Provide similar guidance to audio books: Encourage students to use "the pause" for actively engaging with their audio reading (see The Podcast Pause section in chapter 3), and recommend they create one note or document in their note-taking app for each audio book they are reading for class.

In addition to these texts students must acquire, the professor has also provided select excerpts as PDFs on the LMS. The fluid learning analysis and digital accessibility checklist in chapter 10 would help evaluate how accessible these excerpts are. If they are pages scanned from a print book, check the library for accessible e-versions. If there is limited institutional support in remediating readings that do not meet accessibility standards, prompt students to check out these materials early in the semester and reach out to you if they encounter issues.

Travel Narratives on Blogs and Social Media

Blogs and social media accounts could be fascinating additions to the discussion of the travel genre: What tropes persist in digital media? In Hart's own mobile-mindful learning, she might keep an eye out for Instagram accounts that focus on travel, which may coincide with a blog. Similarly, students could identify examples of travel narratives on blogs and social media and compare these contemporary examples to class texts. Students can consult blogs and social media accounts without interacting themselves, which helps students engage without concerns of privacy. Students may surprise us with how often they are willing to dig into such accounts and think about them next to these other narratives since they can access blogs and social media from their phones. Therefore, it may be worth introducing the idea with one or two examples, encouraging students to find and refer to examples in class, which could then culminate in a course project.

Research Project and Oral Presentation

Students could get creative in using mobile devices to create a research project and oral presentation. Research could involve new media such as blogs, social media accounts, and other multimodal ways travelers tell stories to express places and themselves within those places. Their oral presentations could complement these modes of expression, such as podcasts or videos. Branching out of the oral format, students might even create narratives in interactive maps they create on Google Maps. Such options are explored in the Untether the Research Presentation, Create a Map, and Primary Research via Mobile Device activities in chapter 11.

The very nature of travel is in motion, so inviting travel narratives that happen on mobile devices would be a fitting avenue for creative expression. Hart may want to reflect on the literary nature of the course and how the textual analysis and other integral actions of the course might be achieved in multimodal formats. This course is a good example of guiding students in their reading options and how to get the most out of print, digital, and mobile reading (Cohn, 2021).

Case Study: Management Information Systems for Business Students

This required introductory course for business students focuses on using Microsoft Office to organize, manage, and present information for many business purposes. With its emphasis on Word, Excel, Access, and PowerPoint, this skills course requires a lot of work on computers and these specific programs. While Shaun Moore has taught this as a traditional on-campus course, this particular section is taught in a fully asynchronous online format. The course's instructional material and activities include video lessons, textbook readings, practice activities, quizzes, discussion forums, and two exams.

Even though a class about organizing complex data with computer products seems limited in its mobile-mindful options, there are still opportunities to guide students through mobile choices and to integrate mobile options. Even though Office products are largely designed for computer use, students taking a course on using these products should know how they are being used on mobile devices, as Office products have mobile apps. For example, do Office's products suggest a growth in using PowerPoint for microlearning via self-paced narrated slides? Companies are currently promoting services that convert PowerPoint slides to mobile-friendly micro-lessons (e.g., EdApp, Playablo). While the course objectives may focus on desktop software and skills, mobile information will likely tap into this objective: "how information technology will affect their lives as students and future professionals." Additionally, since one learning outcome is to "use the Web to facilitate collaboration and sharing," then there are reasonable opportunities to consider mobile means for collaboration and sharing. Such learning goals are a good example of the need to create fluid learning opportunities between mobile and computer learning. It is good for business students to identify collaboration tools that allow review and conversation on the go.

Required Materials

This course requires a textbook and accompanying courseware (MyITLab). Moore gives helpful guidance on cost- and format-conscious options. He makes it clear that an e-text is a viable option while also offering a print option. Additionally, the MyITLab courseware may offer mobile-friendly materials such as short videos or flashcards. Moore could explore what mobile components are offered in MyITLab, point this out to students, and provide guidance or recommendations on how to use it, if available. The professor makes clear the technical requirements for using Microsoft Office, along with multiple locations where Office 365 is likely available. He may want to touch on Office apps, even if he wants students to steer clear of using them to complete activities.

Communication

Moore makes himself available by email and text, and through virtual student appointments. He could also add that students can send him a message through the Moodle app or Moodle website. He uses a separate forum in Moodle for student questions and answers to make this a space for everyone rather than the professor alone fielding course questions and troubleshooting tech issues. If students have the Moodle mobile app and are subscribed to that forum, they could receive questions on their phones and respond through the app.

Since this course is fully asynchronous, Moore produces short weekly introduction videos that add teacher presence and prepare students for the week ahead. As such, he could offer them on YouTube so that students can easily view them on their phones. These videos are fun and funny, and the professor has commented on how he never gets to enjoy what reactions students have to them. If he were to share them in a more immediate class communication space like Slack or Discord, students could quickly add reactions (e.g., emojis, "likes") and comments, which increases social presence in the course as well.

Moore offers a social forum where he provides a question or prompt that builds class community or applies course concepts in a fun way, such as using Excel to making pixel art. Such a social forum could take off in a class communication space like Slack or Discord. The Mobile-Mindful Class Communication section in chapter 10 provides more ways to explore such options.

Mobile Data Sources

When students are learning to use Excel, they could practice downloading their social media activity data in Excel and analyze the data accordingly, such as is available in LinkedIn and Twitter. They could analyze how often they are accessing these apps on a phone versus a desktop. The Students Digging Into Their Own Data activity (chapter 11) offers examples of how other instructors have had students analyze data created from their mobile activity.

Case Study: Fundamentals of Professional Nursing Practice

This course, taught by two instructors along with clinical faculty, is foundational for nursing students and therefore requires a tremendous amount of work. Students have to both know and apply medical processes while cultivating patient relationships. While the course relies on specific software for simulations, assessments, and other nursing practices, it would be particularly helpful for students to be able to review practice questions on procedures, safety protocols, and nursing theory and principles on mobile devices to significantly increase retrieval practice opportunities.

Explicitly Explaining Tech Device Opportunities and Restrictions

In the Technology Requirements section of the syllabus, the instructors clearly list what hardware and software are needed, even what settings may be needed in a web browser. Among these is the line: "No iPads, tablets, phones, or hotspots are to be used." The instructors could reflect on the restriction of mobile devices: Do they not want these devices to be used in the classroom during class sessions, or do they also not want them used to do coursework? Should these devices never be used for coursework, or are the devices incompatible with certain simulations and other required programs? Once evaluating the use of mobile devices, this statement could be updated to explain how mobile devices should and should not be used. They could focus on mobile learning options, such as audio reading options available by instructor- and publisher-created content.

Narrated Slides Offered in Audio-Only Format

The instructors share their instruction in narrated PowerPoint slides, which they offer in this narrated form, slides only, and audio only. Lynda Poly-Droulard said this is for mobile learning, as her busy nursing students rely on uninterrupted commute time to focus on instruction (personal communication, March 30, 2022). The instructors could think about how to curate the learning with a playlist. Making these available through an audio player may make it easier for students to get to the episode, download it for offline listening, or navigate through the episode if they need to listen to something again. They might also be inspired to add "pauses" where they ask a question with multiple choices to help students realize whether the main points are sinking in for them. Their slides have questions built in, but no audio. They could add audio files for these as well, reading through the questions and answer options (perhaps twice), and then explaining the answer.

Practice Assessments Again and Again

The instructors allow students to retake assessments until reaching a certain grade threshold, which encourages retrieval practice and familiarity with questions and content leading up to high-stakes proctored exams. With how much nursing students have to cover in this course, having these and other modules and quizzes available in a mobile format could greatly increase the number of times students take these assessments. They could explore publisher content for mobile accessibility of review material or assessments, and evaluate whether other existing activities can be carried out on a mobile device. Additionally, they can benefit from frequently watching video demonstrations, recording themselves doing demonstrations, and taking notes or discussing what was done well or could be improved. As the syllabus was written for the potential pivot to online instruction, students would have to complete a validation (i.e., demonstration) as an unlisted YouTube video, so some practice on uploading YouTube videos could help prepare for such a situation or other extenuating circumstance.

What Now?

At this point you may have a sense of what mobile-mindful first steps would work best for you and your students. As the case studies show, reviewing your syllabi with a mobile-mindful lens may help you identify good areas to start. The next two chapters provide ways to spring into action, starting with Course Planning Activities to customize mobile-mindful learning to your context and then Teaching and Learning Activities you can start using in class.

Reference

Cohn, J. (2021). *Skim, dive, surface: Teaching digital reading.* West Virginia University Press.

COURSE PLANNING ACTIVITIES

After exploring the "why" and "how" of mobile-mindful teaching and learning, let's start to explore what mobile opportunities there are and could be in your courses. These activities can help you evaluate your current courses, apply mobile-mindfulness to core instructional materials and practices, explore apps to include in courses, and communicate with students to ensure mobile options best fit their needs. To practice our mobile learning skills and make these activities as applicable as possible, take advantage of activity templates and other web resources offered in this chapter via QR code or weblink, which will often give you an interactive version of these activities that you can save and adapt.

Check Your Knowledge on Fluid Learning

Fluid learning is being able to carry out a learning activity across devices, time, and space seamlessly (Fang, 2014). Fluid learning is defined by five characteristics:

- neutrality: works well on any device
- granularity: can be consumed in smaller units
- portability: used across platforms
- interactivity: potential connection among others
- ubiquity: learning beyond devices, existing everywhere

How can learning activities include some or all of these five characteristics? Let's start with applying fluid learning characteristics to learning activities from different disciplines:

1. *Recall regions of the brain and their function as it relates to biological psychology.* This recall activity benefits from mobile-friendly flashcards (granular) on apps like Quizlet and Anki.
2. *Compare and contrast impeachments in American history.* This task could rely on the material of history scholars communicating to a wider audience through articles (granular, neutral) and podcasts (portable).
3. *Analyze ways in which public spaces encourage and discourage specific behaviors.* Since this activity encourages place-based learning, ubiquitous learning components come to the forefront. By encouraging students to take photos and share them with one another in a shared photo album, students could also analyze one another's examples (interactive).
4. *Identify the differences between consensus-building and polarizing communication.* This task can draw on news articles (granular, neutral) for an explanation of how these communication styles differ, and students can identify where they occur in social media interactions (interactive, ubiquitous).

With these examples in mind, brainstorm ways to extend learning opportunities related to your course, including on mobile devices. Pick a few learning outcomes or activities from your courses, match them to relevant fluid learning principles, and consider how these could best fit learning with a mobile device.

Fluid Learning Analysis of Your Course

Using your syllabus, evaluate current learning materials for fluid learning or a learner's ability to access and connect learning across different modes and devices (Fang, 2014). A simple method could include noting whether each reading, multimodal instructional material (e.g., lecture video, podcast, narrated slides), in-class activity, and assessment is available in a print, computer, or mobile format. Go through your course on your phone, noting what works and doesn't work well on a phone. Then, make additional notes how each item could expand fluid learning opportunities while maintaining the learning purpose and outcomes. You can access a basic, adaptable worksheet as a starting point by going to christinamoorephd.com/MobileMindful or scanning the QR code (see Figure 10.1).

If this seems overwhelming, start with evaluating two items in each of these categories, perhaps two that are good candidates for increasing fluid learning options or are most frequent in the course. For example, if you

Figure 10.1. QR code to access fluid learning analysis worksheet.

commonly use a survey tool in your LMS, evaluating and adjusting this activity will have a greater impact than a single activity or reading. Starting with select materials may help guide the rest of your course decisions. Appendix A offers an example of how one could evaluate their course materials.

Mobile-Mindful Syllabus

Students tend to receive little guidance in how to best use the digital learning methods available to them, much less those on a phone (Cohn, 2016; Cohn, 2021). Therefore, once you have evaluated your course for fluid learning opportunities and implemented mobile-mindful options, it will go a long way to make these options explicit and provide recommendations and resources on how to use mobile-mindful options well. The following are a few suggestions and language you could use in your syllabus. For a digital copy of this list, visit christinamoorephd.com/MobileMindfulTeaching or scan the following QR code (see Figure 10.2).

Figure 10.2. QR code to access mobile-mindful syllabus list.

Syllabus Format

Is the syllabus in a format that can be accessed on a phone? Can students navigate to key information such as due dates and your contact information? Are hyperlinks to relevant information provided, and is that information mobile-accessible?

Course Texts

Indicate format options for the texts, whether they are available in print, electronically, or both. Is the e-version mobile-accessible? If so, what are the best ways to use the mobile content, or what mobile content would you discourage based on functionality and learning goals? Explicit descriptions and guidance on how to make the best of available formats can ensure students "do the reading" and engage with the content frequently. If your texts include multimodal content (e.g., videos, podcast episodes, photo albums), link students to playlists they can save for easy access throughout the course.

Tech Support

Share what support is available to students at your institution, such as help with the LMS, support for other campus software (e.g., help desk), nearby computer labs, and where students may be able to borrow devices, such as through the student technology center or library. You may also want to include information about how to access wireless internet or programs to which they may have free access. Reminding students of this information early in the term can prompt students to set up technology and accounts, troubleshoot with the right people, and find alternatives if they experience technical difficulties.

Tech Policy

If you have a tech policy, avoid an outright tech ban. Such bans discriminate against students with disabilities and students using e-versions of texts, which are often female students and students of color (Galanek et al., 2018). Describe when and how technology could be conducive to class activities, and when they might be more distracting than beneficial. You might include recommendations such as keeping phones silent or other actions that can reduce distraction. If your class relies on the use of technology, encourage students to bring available devices while describing other options for students, such as print alternatives or where students may be able to borrow devices, such as through the student technology center or library.

Recommended Apps

Listing apps you think will help students boost their mobile learning can help students think about course concepts more often. List the app with a very short description of how they could use the app in conjunction with course activities. Describe these apps as recommended, but not required. If you are requiring an app, explain why it is required and link to information on how students can customize settings related to privacy and notifications. These are some apps you might recommend, among others:

- LMS app, if available (e.g., Moodle, Canvas)
- video conferencing app, for virtual office hours, online class sessions, and meeting with groups (e.g., Zoom, Google Meet)
- task managing app (e.g., Todoist, Google Tasks)
- document creation and sharing app (e.g., Google Drive, Microsoft Word or Teams)
- flashcard app, especially if you have flashcards for students or previous students have shared their flashcards (e.g., Quizlet, Anki)
- communication space, if you are facilitating a space for students to talk to one another and you (e.g., Slack, Discord, GroupMe; you could ask students if they have interest in such a space before setting one up, or students might set one up for themselves)
- video or audio app, if you have videos on a specific platform (e.g., YouTube or Vimeo, Google Podcasts or Spotify)
- photo sharing app, if assignments and projects might call for sharing and curating photos (e.g., Google Photos, Flickr)

If social media is an important component of the course, you may want to list an app accordingly, but be sure to explain options for students who may be hesitant to use these apps, such as ways they can access content without creating a personal account or ways to maintain their privacy.

The recommended apps might only be a few, and the class can work together to add to this list. The Mobile Learning Kit course activity in chapter 11 offers a format for students assembling their own collection of recommended apps.

Mobile-Mindful Class Communication

Most college students are not frequently checking their email and are more inclined to rely on their phones to receive timely messages. If you want to increase the likelihood students will read your messages and tend to them more promptly, it's worth considering mobile-mindful ways to communicate with them.

One-Way Communications From You

LMS apps are useful for notifying students whenever you add a post to an announcements forum. In one click students will be directed to your message, while also still emailing all students, including those who have not opted to use the LMS app. Instructors have opted for other apps such as Remind to send one-way messages. To avoid relying on students using specific apps, my colleague Helena Riha (2017), who teaches linguistics, sends messages to students' phone numbers, which they receive as text messages. She does this as an SMS gateway—an email address with the recipient's cellphone number and carrier in it. The recipient's cellphone number is followed by the carrier's gateway (e.g., 555123456@txt.att.net). After gathering student phone numbers and carriers through a simple optional form, she compiles a mailing list. From there she copy-pastes the list into the BCC cell of email messages to be sent out as texts.

Class Communication Spaces

If your institution has an instructional designer or academic technologist, it may be helpful to ask them to walk through various options for class communication spaces, which will likely include the LMS plus a couple of other options. We have discussed how spaces like Slack and Discord offer more social presence and customization, and academic tech professionals may offer guidance on how to choose such spaces and set them up. They may even give you a head start on materials and tutorials for supporting students in setting up such programs.

While an LMS might not be as fun and interactive as other communication platforms, students will be familiar with the space and can often get mobile notifications for certain messages. As with the business class case study in chapter 9, some classes have a Q & A forum for students and the professor to encourage helping behavior within the community. He could encourage students to subscribe to the forum and add that students can unsubscribe from the whole forum or individual threads.

If you go with a channel-based messaging space like Slack, Discord, or Teams, you will have more decisions to make, which you may want to discuss with students:

1. Will students need to be required to use this space to receive relevant class announcements? If so, what channels will they be required to follow?
2. What channels will you set up? Channels are separate discussion spaces within a whole workspace, which can be organized for specific people or needs.

3. Will students be allowed to create their own channels based on their interests or for their small groups, or will they need to request you to create them?

4. What parameters will you set around notification times? Will you have community timelines and standards, or will all be prompted to set their own preferences?

Student-Informed Mobile Learning

Throughout the book we bring our mobile-mindful teaching ideas back to what students want and need. Since this is the whole purpose of adding mobile learning options, we want to actively include students in our decision-making about mobile-mindful learning rather than make assumptions. Whether in a quick survey at the beginning of the semester or in occasional discussions before class starts, ask them questions like these to not only gather useful data for your teaching but also prompt students to start thinking of themselves as mobile learners.

1. When and why do you use your phone for classes and learning generally?
2. Do you think you can learn well on a phone? What types of mobile learning activities do you think work well, and which ones don't?
3. What apps do you think help you succeed in school?
4. Are you content with how you use your phone? In other words, do you think you use your phone in a healthy, productive way, or do you feel like you waste your time in a way that you wish you didn't?
5. Do you have reliable internet access? Do you rely on your phone as a backup device when you lack other internet access or devices?
6. How likely are you to seek e-versions of required texts? Do you access these on your phones, or would you like to?
7. What kind of class notifications would you like to receive? What notification frequency works best?
8. If you have a question about the course, what is the most effective way for you to ask?
9. If you were sent nongraded review questions and activities you could do on your phone twice a week, 2–3 minutes each time, would you do them?
10. How do you feel about using phones in classrooms? Do you like the idea of participating on your phone to answer questions, or would you find this distracting?
11. Would you have concerns about actively using phones for learning such as your tech literacy, phone capability, and privacy?

Evaluating an App for Instructional Use

If you have "started with self" and previously used an app you would like to integrate into your course, you may already have a sense of the app's relevance, usability, and fluid learning capabilities. Nevertheless, your experience may not automatically account for other important considerations when asking students to use the app, such as its accessibility, storage and hardware requirements, and available support. Therefore, it helps to use a list of considerations to evaluate any app you ask students to download.

University of Central Florida's (UCF) Center for Distributed Learning offers a Mobile Checklist Critique-at-a-Glance, which asks yes/no questions about an app.

- description
- features
- cost
- reviews and ratings
- privacy
- web and phone alternatives
- support
- hardware
- storage
- versions and updates

Upon completion, the webform provides feedback on your selections to guide the implementation of such apps. For example, when I answered "yes" to whether the app is available on multiple phone operating systems (iPhone, Android), the feedback offered, "The app is available on multiple devices! That's great. Make sure to know the differences in the app from one device to another. Often functionality differs even if the app is available for multiple devices." Additionally, a full Mobile App Checklist comes at the end of the form results, which provides more prompting questions related to evaluating an app for student use such as appropriateness, accessibility, security, usability, feedback, and value.

To view UCF's checklist and resulting feedback and guidance, visit https://digitallearning.ucf.edu/msi/staticfiles/mobile-checklist/ or use the following QR code (see Figure 10.3).

As with any checklist or guide shared in this book, adapt it to make it your own by considering your personal, instructional, and institutional context. While this checklist covers many of the fluid learning principles informing this book's mobile-mindful approach, such as availability on different

Figure 10.3. QR code to access UCF's checklist.

types of phones and on a computer, I would add to this list the ability to work offline or how much bandwidth the app requires. While UCF's form is useful for any instructor, some recommendations direct instructors to UCF-specific resources such as FERPA policy, so consider what institutional policies, resources, and people are worth consulting.

If you have students do their own app exploration as I shared in the Mobile Learning Kit in chapter 11, you could share this checklist with students as well.

Thrown Into Learning: Action Before Instruction

Normally learning in the classroom starts with delivery—reading before discussion, lecture before practice, review before testing—when it might be advantageous to flip this order. By asking students to demonstrate knowledge before you have delivered course content via lecture, text, or instructional video, students can better appreciate the gap of knowledge before and after reviewing the course content. By going through the active experience of learning without all of the answers, students are more aware of what they do not know, learn through mistakes, and develop curiosity. Consider when and how you can throw students into learning by starting with hands-on experience before content delivery.

Multistage online discussion forums can be a powerful tool for applying this interpretation of Kolb's (1984) experiential learning model, as students see how their thinking has evolved with more information (Franchini, 2019). These elements all point to an excellent mobile learning opportunity, since we are prompting students to apply their current knowledge in a quick, low-stakes way. Here are a few of many ways you could apply these learning principles to a mobile-mindful learning environment:

1. Send students a survey with questions related to the upcoming unit. It could consist of multiple choice questions only or also open answers. You can use these answers to understand where students are at and show students when they clearly understood a concept and when they did not. Taking the survey less than a day ahead of when the unit will be introduced will make the experience more present in students' minds.
2. Facilitate a discussion about beliefs and experiences related to a unit. A "slow chat" model (described more in chapter 11) is one way to do this with a mobile-mindful approach.
3. Send students a scenario to read and respond to ahead of a class session.

Assessing Our Digital Accessibility Practices

When using any digital medium, following accessibility principles will help ensure content can be used by anyone across different devices, including mobile devices. Use this checklist to gauge your progress on creating accessible digital content and set goals for adopting accessibility practices. This is not an exhaustive list of accessibility actions to consider, but this list provides a foundation that comprises often used instructional content. The goal is not necessarily to check every box, as some items may not apply to your course. For a digital, adaptable version of this checklist with links to related resources, visit christinamoorephd.com/MobileMindful or scan the following QR code (see Figure 10.4).

Figure 10.4. QR code to access digital accessibility checklist.

Inclusive Environment

- I make my syllabus available to students at least a week before a semester begins.
- My syllabus encourages students who may qualify for ADA accommodations to work with the disability support services available at the institution.

- I make some class material available to students ahead of time.
- In at least one assignment, students have multiple choices in content (topic they write about, idea they test) or format (essay, blog, presentation, video).
- I have discussed accessibility issues with students in class (e.g., web accessibility, accessibility in the discipline or career field).
- I have evaluated the extent to which learning materials can be accessed in multiple modes and devices (see the Fluid Learning Analysis earlier in this chapter).

Text Formatting

- I use plain text styles and use 12 point or larger in documents.
- I use plain text styles and use 24 point or larger in slides.
- If I color-code content, I also use text to signify meaning (e.g., if blue font indicates optional activities, I also put the word OPTIONAL in front of the blue font).
- I share weblinks by hyperlinking text that describes the web location (e.g., "Digital Accessibility Quick Note" rather than "Click here" or "https://docs.google.com/document/d/1Nlm_5cDhpsgmn2lfu4uWrnL y0js0BaYxCdnWIIhRcpw/edit?usp=sharing").

Documents and Slides

- I have used heading styles for section titles in a document or webpage.
- I have run a file through an accessibility checker.
- I have used an accessibility checker to fix accessibility issues.
- I use the program's formatting tools to organize content rather than manually insert spaces (e.g., indents, bulleted lists, alignment, line and section spacing).
- I have offered students course files in multiple formats (e.g., assignment description in PDF and Word).
- I have identified PDFs that may pose accessibility challenges (e.g., book scans, blurry text files).
- I have found a more accessible alternative to a PDF file I previously used.
- My slides use high color contrast.
- Slides use designated title and text boxes.

Images and Videos

- I know what alt text for images is, and I know when it is necessary.
- I have added alt text to an image.

- I have simplified my use of images for clarity (e.g., using plain text instead of a screenshot of text).
- I have considered accessibility guidelines when creating a complex image like a graph, chart, or table.
- I have altered practices of how I use complex images to increase accessibility (e.g., created an alternative linear format for a table or graph, added alt text to a diagram).
- I have accurate captions for at least one of my instructional videos.
- I have shared a transcript of at least one of my original instructional videos or audio files.

External Content

- I regularly check weblinks to make sure they are not broken (i.e., they go to the intended location).
- When I link students to an external website, I have done a spot-check for accessibility issues (sufficient color contrast, flexible text format).
- Before including videos in my course, I check whether the video has accurate captions.

Recommendations When Requiring or Strongly Encouraging Social Media for a Course

In a workshop I attended on using social media in teaching, someone asked if we as instructors can require students to use social media for a course activity. The question made me realize that we force students to use lots of technology such as LMS, blogs, e-proctoring programs, e-texts, courseware, and simulations. Some are vetted by colleges and universities, such as the LMS, but others are minimally vetted or not at all. While I offer these recommendations for preparing a class to use social media safely and responsibly, I would recommend similar practices with adopting other educational technologies. Whenever we require students to use technology, we should also take responsibility for informing and supporting students in their use and sharing that responsibility with the tech experts at our institutions.

- *Explain the rationale for using a certain social media platform* to meet the course's learning outcomes in a way that would be difficult to do without social media.

- *Provide students the support they need*: descriptions, instructions, demos, tutorials, and potentially support on campus. You can lean on support materials from social media platforms, customizing as needed for your class purposes.
- *Tend to ethical considerations*, such as the information the social media platforms collect and how to limit such collecting, such as tracking their location using activity to push advertisements to connected platforms. Similarly, make clear how students can protect their privacy, limit notifications, delete content, and block others.
- *Explicitly discuss challenges related to social media*, such as privacy and information literacy, and how to build skills that mitigate potential issues.
- *Monitor student accounts* to get an early assessment of whether students are understanding and implementing recommendations and provide feedback if any content is concerning.
- *Check in with students and encourage their feedback.*

End-of-Semester Curation, Reflection, and Management of Mobile Learning Activity

At the end of a course, students show what they have learned through cumulative assessments. Sometimes we also conclude courses with how students can transfer and apply what they have learned beyond the course. In addition to this type of reflection activity, we could also prompt students to do some practical curation of course activities and resources, and do some digital cleanup.

In the final week of my writing courses, students selected the top five resources from the course (e.g., readings, guides, activities), annotating briefly what was useful about that resource and how they anticipated using it in future contexts. In doing so, they also downloaded those materials or saved the links, serving as a reminder that their LMS course access would eventually expire. Without an intentional process for labeling and storing course content, course materials and students' hard work may "languish in a temporary Downloads file in the internet browser" (Cohn, 2021, p. 269). The issue is compounded on our phones, where content tends to be even more fleeting. Taking a fluid learning approach will help: If students are using tools linked across devices, then it is more likely that course-related content is linked to accounts rather than devices. Nevertheless, it is crucial students make sense of all of the material they have produced as a result of their courses and decide what to do with it.

Let's say a student gravitated toward mobile note-taking and created many notes in Google Keep, each 20–200 words. Near the end of the semester, she is staring down many notes, none of them labeled. At this point labels may not be helpful, as she may ultimately want the notes to live outside of this app. She could download each note as a Google Doc, although this would create a lot of short Google Docs. Instead she might settle on copy-pasting the note content into one doc, deleting some notes along the way. In doing so, she is reviewing her evolving thoughts dictated in fits and spurts, and can organize them to create a single picture of the course.

Along with directing students to intentionally save their material, we will also want to empower them to delete work and activity.

- *Inform students of how long they and you will maintain access to the LMS's course pages.* If you collect work outside of the LMS or download work from the LMS, tell students how long you will hold onto their work before deleting it.
- *Remind students they can delete any app they used during the course,* whether it was required or recommended. Deleting could save space on their phones.
- *Before deleting, recommend students confirm that any information they want to keep is saved somewhere else.*
- *For class communication spaces outside of the LMS, either delete the space or talk with students about what the procedure should be for maintaining the space.* In any case, students should easily be able to opt out of the space.

These are reminders for us as instructors as well to properly curate data as needed, but not hold onto student work any longer than necessary.

References

Cohn, J. (2016). "Devilish smartphones" and the "stone-cold" Internet: Implications of the technology addiction trope in college student digital literacy narratives. *Computers and Composition, 42,* 80–94. https://doi.org/10.1016/j.compcom.2016.08.008

Cohn, J. (2021). *Skim, dive, surface: Teaching digital reading.* West Virginia University Press.

Fang, B. (2014, October 13). Creating a fluid learning environment. *EDUCAUSE Review.* https://er.educause.edu/articles/2014/10/creating-a-fluid-learning-environment

Franchini, B. (2019, October). *Using online discussion sequences to change student thinking.* The Lilly Conference on Teaching and Learning – Traverse City. https://www.lillyconferences-mi.com/

Kolb, D. A. (1984). *Experiential learning: Experience as the source of learning and development.* Prentice Hall.

Riha, H. (2017). Communicate with class texts. *Teaching Tips Blog.* Center for Excellence in Teaching and Learning, Oakland University. https://oakland.edu/cetl/teaching-resources/teaching-tips/2017/Communicate-with-Class-Texts

II

TEACHING AND
LEARNING ACTIVITIES

After preparing a course for mobile-mindful learning opportunities, you can begin thinking about what activities you and students can do. These activities have been organized into four areas: building mobile learning skills, class engagement, community engagement, and student research with mobile devices. While the activities remain fluid across devices, they focus on particularly mobile-friendly learning actions. Some activities can be adapted to a variety of class types, while others will give you a starting point to develop activities specific to your discipline and needs. To practice our mobile learning skills and make these activities as applicable as possible, take advantage of activity templates and other web resources offered via QR code or weblink, which will often give you an interactive version of these activities that you can save and adapt.

Building Mobile Learning Skills

These activities encourage students to be intentional mobile learners, both directly related to your courses and in any learning endeavor.

Mobile Learning Kit

The Mobile Learning Kit project is a great way to collaboratively explore and experience mobile tech as it relates to the specific course or college learning generally. In this activity, student teams put together a mobile learning kit that would help them accomplish the course learning outcomes (Moore, 2016). Have students choose up to 15 apps and organize them into three or four categories by theme, task, or course learning outcome. Provide a low hypothetical budget in order to encourage free app discovery while allowing an occasional paid app if it seems valuable or necessary (suggested total budget: $15). Students describe each app and how it relates to the work of the course. Students can also use UCF's Mobile Checklist Critique-at-a-Glance form to evaluate app usability (see Evaluating an App for Instructional Use in chapter 10). I had students organize their app categories and choices in a table format, but there are plenty of other ways for the mobile learning kit to be communicated.

In my implementation, which I called the Mobile Composition Kit since I teach writing, the project spanned 1 week, which included a pre-project discussion on discipline-related technologies across decades and a post-project discussion on mobile technology's place in today's discipline or in learning generally.

The Mobile Learning Kit project achieves the following outcomes:

1. Discuss with students transfer for course skills, pre- and post-project.
2. Reflect on the cumulative skills of the course.
3. Assess how students perceive the work of the course and the discipline or field generally.
4. Build a Mobile Learning Kit for future courses.
5. Evaluate how mobile learning could work in course content.

While I have used this as an end-of-semester assignment for students to reflect on learning outcomes and how they perceive skills and work related to the course, it could also be introduced earlier. By doing this at the beginning of the semester, students can put these mobile learning kits to use, reflect on their usefulness throughout the course, and make adjustments accordingly.

Regardless of whether students envision using mobile tech in their course or discipline, this activity prompts students to define the skills and tools of the trade. When a student has to think through the mobile app tools that would be helpful to a social worker, a microbiologist, or an industrial engineer, they have to think about the day-to-day actions of these professionals. If taking photos are important, what do they need to do with those photos, and which apps best achieve that purpose? Students in my first-year writing courses thought about what it means to be a writer and revealed to me how they envisioned this work. Such Mobile Learning Kits may even be useful to future students. You might decide to include a list of recommended apps in the syllabus explaining how they could support learners in the course.

Students worked in teams to make the kit-building process collaborative and iterative, but it also allowed flexibility if some students did not have mobile devices or were not comfortable downloading certain apps. While downloading free apps helps students test out the functionality, downloading apps was not required for this activity. Making actual mobile app access and use optional is mindful of the "ethics" category of the M-COPE framework (Dennen & Hao, 2014).

To view an example assignment description for this activity, scan the following QR code (see Figure 11.1) or visit christinamoorephd.com/MobileMindful.

Figure 11.1. QR code to access example mobile learning kit.

Note: I originally shared the Mobile Learning Kit project in the book chapter "Making a Mobile Composition Kit: Project for Testing the Waters." Description of this project and its learning outcomes have been reprinted with permission from the National Council of Teachers of English, Copyright 2016.

Cultivating a Learning Ecology

A learning ecology recognizes the many different contexts where learning happens and how these contexts are or should be connected. This idea acknowledges that learning happens beyond credits at a school. It also encourages the diversity of an interconnected learning environment. Throughout a course, have students recognize where one can learn about the concepts related to the course, the strengths of these sources and perspectives, and how they fit with other types of information and the broader scheme of the discipline or profession. Students should cultivate their learning ecologies based on their needs, interests, goals, and strengths. In doing this, students can take one unit they were fascinated with from the course and let it flourish in multiple learning venues. If a student in a global health class is an elementary education major, they may gear their ecologies toward elementary educators' blogs and YouTube accounts. Their classmate may be a communications major who focuses on communication strategies among different countries.

Have students cultivate a learning ecology and curate its elements. Such a project adapts the ePortfolio idea to focus on what informs one's individual learning rather than just what they produce for a course. Have them organize whom they learn from, what these people add to the learning ecology, and even reflect on what type of learning is most valuable to them and where they could diversify even more. Based on your teaching philosophy and student audience, you may want to let students do this however they see fit. If you would prefer to start them with a structure that they can adapt, provide a starter document of learning sources. Students can remove what is not of interest, add more to specific areas, add new categories, and keep pruning and growing the environment accordingly.

Throughout the semester, have students share how they have been adapting that initial list and what they have learned through this cultivation.

1. Do they find they are learning through lecture or demonstration videos they have organized into a playlist?
2. If they have been learning from people on Twitter, have they curated them into a Twitter list that organizes those voices and allows them to share the list with others?
3. How are they capturing and applying what they have learned from these sources? Are they creating videos of their own that they post to TikTok? Are they writing their own blog posts in response to other bloggers, even if they are keeping them unpublished as they decide whether to make those thoughts public?

By having students share and articulate the process of learning throughout the semester, you are encouraging lifelong learning behaviors and different ways of knowing that will help them bring more motivation and creativity to class activities.

When students share their materials, students can add to their learning ecologies based on one another's. They might even contribute to a shared class document or forum so that future classes can benefit.

Example

As an educational developer, I have created teaching and learning collections (Moore, n.d.) that work in this way and can be used as a model for what you might create for your courses. These Google Docs curate learning materials based on a teaching topic, such as trauma-informed teaching, reading and writing, and digital accessibility. The materials are organized by mode: articles, research, videos, books, even whom to follow on Twitter. Some categories focus on what comes from the institution, situating the topic in our immediate context. In one click users can make a copy of this collection and begin deleting, adding, and annotating.

Issue a Mobile Learning Challenge

Depending on the amount of learning material in your course that you have vetted for mobile-mindfulness, issue students a Mobile Learning Challenge with small, feasible, and beneficial steps. The challenge could be for students to access your course's learning material at least twice a day for 7 days. Have students complete a daily log of what they did each day, submit this to you and, preferably, discuss it as a class. With the Mobile Learning Challenge instructions, provide options for how students can log their daily activity on their phones, or discuss possibilities with students as a group. Provide prompts like these to develop information and feedback most beneficial for you and for them:

1. How long did you normally spend on a learning task? What was the shortest and longest amount of time you spent?
2. What type of learning activity worked best on your phone?
3. What type of learning activity did you avoid on your phone, and why?
4. Did your mobile learning activity flow into your desktop/laptop and offline learning activity?
5. What type of learning activity did you create apart from the course materials (e.g., separate note-taking doc)?

Since the goal of such a challenge is for students to participate in your mobile-mindful pedagogy and learn how to be mobile learners, such an activity should be required, but either as ungraded or as complete/incomplete.

Mobile Scavenger Hunt

Scavenger hunts have long been used in college courses as an experiential learning activity, and plenty of instructors have taken advantage of smartphones to include photos and videos in the scavenger hunt. Scavenger hunts can either get students physically moving around a campus, moving around another area, or even doing a completely web-based scavenger hunt.

Taking photos and videos is a simple task, but you will need to organize how those items are curated and collected, whether it is in a shared Google Photos album, Google Drive folder, Slack channel, or class Flickr account. Accounting for the portability component of fluid learning, use a method that is easy to view on other devices, such as if students are to show these photos to the class on a projector or share them in a discussion forum via the LMS.

1. *Course concepts in the wild.* Have students find examples of course concepts in a specific location or in students' everyday places.
2. *The places of your discipline.* If classes meet on campus, write a scavenger hunt that takes students to the places you and past students have deemed important for the course such as a special collection or archives at the library, the art gallery, and the student technology center. This is especially important for online courses: Have students find a specific title in the online course catalog or take a screenshot of where they can sign up for virtual writing center consultations.
3. *Compare Twitter accounts of people in similar industries.* Since Twitter is a public platform by default, an account is not required to browse tweets (posts on Twitter). Have students identify five people related to your field who are on Twitter and compare how they use Twitter. Are they sharing research, promoting their publications, engaging others in conversation, or making arguments? Students with Twitter accounts can "follow" these people, which makes it easier to keep up with them. Have students view their activity over time, save screenshots of or links to notable tweets, and share their analysis in a written paper, presentation, or discussion forum. After students have shared their analysis, you or your students can create a Twitter list that curates all of these people and allows users to view tweets only from these people.

Class Engagement

These activities engage students with one another and you during a class session and keeps the class connected beyond set course times.

Wrap the Class Session With Short Surveys
Before class or after class, use simple forms or surveys for review, quizzes, check-ins, and muddiest points using survey apps like Google Forms and

Qualtrics. Students can complete these in the moments leading up to class time, and you can show the results immediately, as appropriate. If you use a projector, you can project a QR code and URL. Additionally, you can send this information to students an hour before class. Some options include:

1. Leading up to class, ask students to write a two-sentence summary of the last class session or the reading students did for homework.
2. Ask students five multiple choice or short answer questions related to past lesson content. Alternatively, ask students questions related to the class session ahead, which can activate prior knowledge, pique curiosity, and show students what they have to learn that day. (Additionally, you could have students take the same quiz at the end of the session to see if their answers have changed based on the session.)
3. Use the same simple form at the end of class sessions to prompt meta-cognition and reflection. Such a form could ask for a four-sentence summary of the class, the top thing they learned or thought about, or the question they have and concept that they still struggle with (also known as "muddiest point").

As for all learning environments, it is best to know the technology context for your class: what type of technology students can access in class, whether the classroom has strong enough internet access for these activities, and so on. Plan for flexibility: Providing links allows students with laptops to access forms, and having a stack of index cards at the front of the classroom gives students a handwritten option. If anonymity is important to activities and undermined by class dynamics, have students keep their own assessments or have a pencil-and-paper backup option.

Sending "Did You Know?" Syllabus-Based Reminders

While we regard the syllabus as a crucial course guide to be used throughout the semester, we tend to give it a lot of attention at the beginning of the semester and then only refer to the schedule and due dates throughout the semester. Syllabi tend to include a lot of helpful information, some of which is useful at specific times and in specific situations and others that are useful throughout the semester. To make this information more visible and timely for students, plot out the course's policies and supports, and 1 or 2 weeks that would be great for sharing a reminder with students focusing on one of these items at a time. There are many ways to do this that are either completely in your control or created with students:

1. *Reserve the first 2 minutes of class to share this reminder.* Students can hear from your voice and body language what this service or policy is and how it will most likely affect and help them. Doing so in a live class session gives them a chance to ask a question. By continually directing students to the syllabus for more information, you are reinforcing its importance throughout the semester.

2. *Include the reminder in a weekly message.* If you regularly send messages as emails, videos, or something else, include briefly one of these reminders. If you use a mobile-friendly communication option such as the LMS app or Remind, you may be able to include these reminders as a separate message, linking students to the syllabus.

3. *Create a slide or digital "card" with the reminder.* Create a slide presentation just for these reminders and have one slide displayed in the minutes leading up to class. Make the message brief enough to be visible at every spot in the room, and include a QR code to relevant links, forms, or the syllabus. If you use social media or photo sharing in your course, create mobile-friendly cards with these reminders. Both formats can be used from semester to semester with minimal tweaks.

4. *Involve students in the reminder process.* Rather than reading the syllabus at the beginning of the semester, have students determine what policies and syllabus material would be helpful reminders, when they should be timed, and what the reminder format and process should be. Students can even create and write the texts, slides, or cards.

Create a Guide to Collaborative Technologies

This activity is adapted from Barton and Klint's (2011) *Writing Spaces* book chapter on strategically using collaborative technologies in student teamwork. As with all of its book chapters, this chapter is written for a student audience. Barton and Klint use a social process narrative to imagine the ups and downs of collaboration: how students will stay connected and build off of one another's ideas, how they will confirm understanding of expectations, what happens when a teammate is struggling or gets delayed, and how they will check in with one another. This narrative is then complemented with what technology tools can facilitate this process such as tools for group conversation, curating sources and ideas, writing collaboratively, and connecting to the instructor. They are mindful of how mobile technologies can help students stay connected to one another and use small learning moments on social media to build ideas together in the prewriting stage of collaborative writing. While the technologies highlighted in their chapter have aged, you could prompt student teams to make their own guide to collaborative technologies. You could use this description as a starting point:

> Since we have limited time to talk with one another in the classroom, we will want to plan for how student teams will communicate with one another, keep track of tasks, organize project materials, and check in on progress. To get the most out of team work, each group will create a collaborative technologies guide, which includes the tasks you will need to accomplish, challenges and opportunities that may arise, and the technologies that will best help you work well as a team. In your collaborative technologies guide, identify what tasks you will need to coordinate and which tools will best facilitate this work. Favor tools that work across devices (in other words, programs you can use well on a phone and computer, and with different phone types). Identify apps that may help in communication and idea generation, and how you can curate ideas and sources in a shared storage space. Consider what challenges may occur along the way based on your past teamwork experiences and talk through a process that will help keep everyone on track.

When I taught first-year composition students, team projects started with a proposal to ensure students had a proactive plan. The proposal included a collaborative technologies guide like this. Such a guide helps students plan for fluid learning, including which apps they may want to download and how their communication and prewriting will ultimately lead into collaborative writing.

A Class "Slow Chat"

"Slow chats" are an interactive, "sychron-ish" (Sean Michael Morris in St. Amour, 2020) discussion design popular on Twitter Chats. Discussion facilitators post five questions over 1 hour inviting anyone to respond to these questions, organizing related posts with a hashtag and question/answer labels like "Q1, Q2" and "A1, A2." Slow chats bring people together for what feels like a live discussion without requiring people to have totally focused attention over that hour period, although many who participate in a slow chat end up spending the whole hour answering questions, reading posts, and replying accordingly. This model also allows people to only read and listen, and for people to follow up on the discussion later if they were unavailable during that hour. Slow chats work particularly well for mobile engagement, but also work well on laptops and desktops. In my digital ethnography on teaching development in social online spaces, some interview participants preferred slow chats to Zoom discussions because they could engage in a discussion while taking care of children (Moore, 2021).

Instead of a traditional post-once-reply-twice discussion forum, facilitate a class slow chat during which you will pose a handful of questions over an hour. Encourage students to do their best to participate in that hour by answering questions and responding to one another's answers. This slow chat model could work well if your course has an online communication space such as Discord or Slack. Discussion platforms with mobile apps allow for timely notifications and easy ways to respond from a phone.

Example: If you are about to discuss social media use in digital identity formation, you might use a slow chat to prompt students to recall stories and practices that might anchor concepts you will discuss in class. Therefore, you might start the chat with something like this:

> Hi, all! We are officially starting the "slow chat," but jump in whenever you can. To answer Q1, start your answer with "A1" so that we can clearly see how your response matches the question. I will post Q1, and then about 15 minutes later I will post Q2.
>
> Q1: How do you choose what to post on your social media accounts? If you don't have social media accounts, why is that?
>
> Q2: How do people's identities tend to change based on the type of social media account they use?

Questions should be short, specific, and provoking, focusing on free responses rather than linking to sources or researching examples (although it is common for slow chat participants to add links to relevant sources and examples). Slow chats like these can help prime the pump for learning academic concepts since they will be able to connect these concepts to actual situations and themselves more readily. Doing a slow chat before introducing concepts will allow you to refer to slow chat examples, making those concepts more accessible and applicable.

Depending on the success and relevance of slow chats, this activity could also be facilitated by students. Small groups can plan out questions ahead of time, schedule the date and time for the chat with the class, and coordinate who will post which questions and actively respond to answers. Since this collaborative process is how many Twitter-based slow chats are facilitated, such experience may equip students to lead Twitter Chats in another context. In the interest of fluid learning, consider allowing participation options for those who are unavailable during the hour or have other challenges in participating. They could contribute a summative action such as reviewing, synthesizing, or curating the discussion.

Community Engagement

Mobile learning's power lies in being able to easily engage people with the community. These activities prompt students to apply course learning within community settings.

Spreading the Word on Campus With QR Codes and Multimodal Messages

Professor of digital rhetoric and multimodal composition Moe Folk (2016) had students compose an audio essay in Audacity, upload it to SoundCloud, create a QR code to the SoundCloud audio piece, and print it on a flier in a strategic location on a college campus. He describes the rhetorical choice as "literacy that goes beyond letteracy," meaning students could more immediately reach their audience than a letter to the editor of a student newspaper (p. 36). In such an assignment, Folk wanted his students to understand the rhetorics of multiple places and modalities, from the physical place where the flier would hang to what audio message would most appeal to the student occupying that space and what other physical space or online place the message would prompt students (e.g., sign a petition, attend an on-campus event).

Such an activity could be adapted for other subjects and purposes. Students could post around campus what they discovered about the plant life on campus to advocate for investment in native plants and the removal of invasive species. This project could use QR codes to link students to audio pieces such as in Folk's assignment or to a captioned photo on Flickr that describes the plant, its contribution or harm to the local ecosystem, and a link to a petition to invest only in native plants. A similar project could be adapted for many other learning contexts, such as increasing awareness of accessibility shortcomings regarding buildings, furniture, technology, and digital content; and describing the architecture of buildings on campus.

Mobile First in the Discipline

While this book is not directly aimed at mobile-first approaches, you may want to give students a sample of mobile-first topics related to your discipline or invite students to consider mobile-first applications of course content.

While she does not embed much mobile learning into her communication and journalism courses, Chiaoning Su includes one class activity on virtual reality (VR) journalism to expose them to emerging journalism trends (personal communication, April 6, 2022). She uses low-cost VR goggles that work with students' smartphones. Through this experience, she has students consider what this new medium adds to journalism, such as the increased empathy readers may have by being more immersed in the source contexts of news stories.

Like Su, you may choose to briefly introduce students to mobile-first approaches in the discipline. You may also invite students to explore the mobile-first practices in which their discipline's work is already engaged. In the early days of the global COVID-19 pandemic, the World Health Organization had to figure out how to most effectively communicate public health information to a massive global audience, and ultimately landed on WhatsApp, a messaging app popular throughout the world (Walwema, 2021). Such a decision reflected an awareness that most of the world's only consistent means of timely information access is through their phones (Pew Research Center, 2019). Even in the United States where people increasingly own multiple internet devices (Pew Research Center, 2021), organizations are leaning into mobile-first learning for professions that need very quick, timely training on rapidly evolving skills (Udalova, 2022).

Prompt your students to consider mobile-first applications in the course or discipline. For example, how might elementary math educators help parents support their children in learning math, especially since Common Core curriculum likely teaches math differently than parents learned it? If the district provides resources, how easy are they to discover and use via parents' mobile devices? The following is a short sample activity description you could adapt for your courses. Add to this description specific relevance to your discipline and how best to share their results and ideas, whether through slides, video, or class discussion. In this sample activity, students are prompted to save and share screenshots, so it would be worth sharing how students can do so or find out how to do so (i.e., what buttons to press and how you recommend students save their screenshots so that they can use them for this activity).

Sample Activity Description for Students

We should be aware of how technological advances affect our professional work, especially how our audience is likely to receive communications. Are stakeholders likely to be mobile phone users? If so, how do they use mobile phones? Which apps do they use, and in what types of situations? Consult data on mobile phone usage by demographic, such as data shared by the Pew Research Center.

Then, evaluate current mobile access for information and services relevant to your stakeholders by navigating key information and organizations on a smartphone. Can someone effectively navigate information, fill out forms, and communicate on a phone? Save screenshots to show examples of effective and ineffective design. (Be sure to save these screenshots somewhere you can access on your computer, such as a photosharing app or cloud storage app.) Then, offer suggestions on how to better design sites and processes for mobile phone users, such as tools to use and how information is organized.

Untether the Research Presentation

Classes often have a presentation component to research, in which the default is often text-heavy presentation slides. Revamp this presentation assignment by encouraging or requiring students to not use slides or to make a presentation that is not restricted to the presentation screen or even the classroom. You can even opt to do away with presentations entirely and instead have students imagine how this information can be used or communicated with a direct audience. Have students come up with an application for their research, essay, or idea such as an app design, social media campaign, an interactive tour, or a video. The "Spreading the Word on Campus" activity is one example of communicating your course-related learning to a wider audience. Many of these options include or focus on mobile outlets.

The following is an example activity description I have used in a research writing course, which resulted in students creating a music video to teach a concept to young children, curating stories and experiences around tattoos in a Facebook Group, writing a children's book, creating a game, and planning a Twitter campaign informing students about the effects of sleep and rest on learning. I originally called this component of the research project "Research in Action," but I like the term "untethering," which Pacansky-Brock and Leafstedt (2016) used to describe learning that happens beyond a set place and time.

Sample Activity: Research in Action

Show the application of the research you have done, including how you can use the knowledge you have created to solve a problem: a lack of a necessary service, a more efficient use of a service, a new process for accomplishing work. The following are a some of many potential ideas:

- website that provides a resource (e.g., tool, guide)
- curriculum for a specific subject that represents a paradigm shift in teaching, learning, or training (a better way to teach a concept, technology use in the classroom)

- social media account/page that serves a purpose among an audience (offers resources, specific ways for people to connect)
- app design
- interactive website that can evaluate people's knowledge or customize an action plan related to an issue
- grant application
- new student organization
- crowdsourced product (draft only)

You will need to draw up a proposal that persuades a set audience to help with funding, provide materials needed to accomplish the task, or whatever the end goal of the product is. If your project requires funding, like those on Kickstarter, you should have specific estimates on what would be required.

Making This Project Happen: Due to the restrictions of a single semester, most of the more complicated projects will have to be boiled down to a proposal and plan, but it should be treated with the seriousness and professionalism with which you would present the idea to a university, local organization, or company. It should be something that could be feasibly accomplished by college students with minimal funding. Be open to moving a project forward beyond the semester: Making these projects a reality is one of the best things you can do for your résumé and future. I am open to advising any effort that you or your team would like to take in putting the project into action beyond the semester. This could include:

- presenting work at a conference
- seeking outlets for your work
- further developing your work

Create or Use a Map

Recognizing motion and place as two elements of mobile learning, we can consider how to create or use maps for learning. Tools like Google Maps can be used to create individual and collaborative maps, which curate information by geographic location. In exploring how university libraries were using Google Maps to share academic information, Dodsworth and Nicholson (2012) noted examples of using Google Maps to digitize historical maps, link photo archives to their geographical location, and curate census data. At a smaller scale, an instructor can use such a map for a campus-wide scavenger hunt. Calling back to the case study on Travel Narratives in Literature in chapter 9, students or instructors could map the routes writers took in composing their travel narratives, providing a visual guide of how often routes overlapped or which areas of the world are more or less traveled.

Online maps like Google Maps allow not only for navigation and copious information about places in the local area, but also for guiding people toward resources. As one example, urban foragers have created collaborative Google Maps in order to mark where to find certain fruits and other edible plants (McIntire-Strasburg, 2021). In line with "Untethering the Research Presentation," encourage students to apply information they learn to create interactive maps not just for the class but for a wider audience as well. Google Earth Education offers resources specifically for teaching, from existing resources for students to use to ways to create maps for educational purposes.

Student Research With Mobile Devices

Mobile devices gather plentiful data, and mobile-mindful students can use these capabilities to conveniently and adeptly gather diverse forms of research.

Students Digging Into Their Own Data

Many tech companies collect loads of user data, some of whom make that data available to users. To increase students' digital literacy and connect course content to everyday contexts, consider how you could use this data collecting for a purpose. One instructor had students practice developing sampling methods and data analytics by having them play Pokémon Go! daily and then downloading and analyzing a week's worth of data in a spreadsheet (Colin et al., 2021). Students could even compile data of technology used in the course, such as the LMS, messaging programs, and social media interactions—data that could be used to develop scholarship of teaching and learning, similar to what faculty at two different institutions did on their analysis of Slack as a class communication space (Alvarez Vazquez et al., 2020). Students could analyze location-based data through GPS tracking, movement-based data in activity tracking apps, phone behavior through their phones' digital well-being apps, and social interactions through social media apps (Dennen & Hao, 2014, p. 413). The activity could either focus on research methods, such as in the Pokémon Go! example, or students could use the data itself to inform a topic.

Students could also analyze existing data-sharing and collecting processes. In teaching rhetoric and critical digital studies, Stephanie Vie (2016) had students critically analyze the terms of service and privacy policies for social network games. She asked students to play a social game on Facebook after reviewing a couple of articles and a TED talk, had the students review the social nature of the games and interactions, and also do a rhetorical analysis of the terms of service and privacy policies.

Such activities not only use rich data sources, but also make students aware of just how much of their data is collected and how it is used. Alongside students, we can decipher "what we see, what we forget to see, and what we are encouraged to not see at all" (Vie, 2016, p. 92). Students develop the ability to see that data, thus giving them the agency to make changes to their preferences and advocate for changes in data collection processes generally.

Primary Research via Mobile Device

By having students use their phone to gather artifacts from their surroundings, we are engaging students in experiential and ubiquitous learning. A phone's tools can either find and record sought-after artifacts or capture research samples as they come up. Just as with any primary research, consider research ethics related to the research context such as informed consent, anonymity, public spaces, and copyrighted content.

1. *Talk with a fellow student in the course.* Have students audio-record conversations with one another about the course content or collaboratively share photos of diagrams they drew of relationships between concepts.
2. *Talk with someone outside of the course.* Interviews recorded through video or audio can serve as a flipped class version of class visitors. Such interviews can also involve the student explaining course concepts to a layperson and having a conversation about how this topic interacts with life outside of academia.
3. *Observation data.* Students can save links and take screenshots for learning or research purposes, such as conversations on social media, phone-based processes, web accessibility shortcomings, or app designs. Students should not use data that is not public such as text messages, closed social media groups, and photos from private gatherings without approval from the Institutional Review Board (IRB).
4. *Survey data.* Have students make a questionnaire with Qualtrics or Google Forms, and have a few sheets with QR codes printed on them so that participants can easily and confidentially take the questionnaire.

These three examples show research methods and activities that work particularly well on a phone and across multiple disciplines and modes.

Primary Research Example: Contribute a Conversation, Gather Research With StoryCorps

This audio-based course activity provides opportunities for students to listen to and contribute stories and use this audio story archive to conduct research. Starting in 2003, StoryCorps was a booth in Grand Central Terminal in New York that invited people to stop in and record their story for posterity (usually a conversation between two people). Now anyone, anywhere can contribute stories that will be curated and archived by the Library of Congress, now totaling over a half million stories. StoryCorps has a website and an app for accessing and recording stories.

1. *Listen to stories.* StoryCorps provides a few types of course activities that can serve a range of disciplines and learning goals. Its stories could be used as part of the learning material in the course, which could be particularly powerful for connecting more abstract, instructive content to the lives of real people. During a unit on learning disabilities, students could listen to Eileen Kushner's story about how she encountered boundaries to work throughout her life and how her husband eventually helped her break through difficulties associated with math ("Larry Kushner and Eileen Kushner," 2016).

2. *Use stories as primary research.* As publicly available stories, StoryCorps material can be used for students' research projects. They could evaluate the stories of math educators such as Ralph Catania to analyze their instructional strategies or relationships with students ("Ralph Catania and Colbert Williams," n.d.). Available transcripts help with this process, allowing students to more easily quote, annotate, and compare wording among multiple interviews. By encouraging students to use existing primary research data, they have the option to engage in primary research that does not involve collecting and producing it themselves.

3. *Contribute stories.* While StoryCorps continues the tradition of having recording booths that interviewees can visit, they have set up their system so that you can record stories from the phone app or with any equipment. As discussed earlier with having students interview one another, students could decide if they want to contribute these stories to StoryCorps.

StoryCorps is one example of other archives that encourage public contributions. Explore other efforts to collect and curate stories, such as oral history projects conducted in your local area. You or your class may even be inspired to create your own space.

Primary Research Example: Follow a Conversation or Movement on Social Media

If students have limited research skills related to collecting their own data, students can use publicly available social media content as a form of primary research. My dissertation was largely based on Twitter data, which branched into other publicly available online data (blogs, videos, events) that I supplemented with interviews.

While areas of social media research are boundless, it may help for students to explore conversations, movements, and experiences as shared on social media—endeavors that are inherently social. As the instructor, you could provide students one to three conversations to follow and analyze based on course topics and your own social media learning. Additionally, you could encourage students to identify social media movements related to the course. Here are three examples:

1. *Climate change activism among American teenagers.* Social media is a powerful tool for activism, especially in areas of the world where governments suppress communication channels crucial for community organization. Students could observe how younger people are leveraging Instagram and TikTok to engage in activism, and what this activism looks like.

2. *Experiences of disabled students and faculty on college campuses.* Groups of people who are underrepresented and marginalized in specific contexts find in widespread social media the opportunity to connect with one another. While younger people might gravitate toward Instagram and TikTok to capture examples of inaccessible physical and digital spaces, faculty and professionals might be more inclined to network on Twitter or organize in semiprivate Facebook Groups.

3. *Public relations strategies among young entrepreneurs.* Such a research scope could involve following a limited number of young entrepreneurs and how they use a range of social media. In my local area, a young developer took to TikTok to crowdsource ideas for filling vacant spots at his newly acquired local mall (Washington, 2022). Other young entrepreneurs might take a different approach on LinkedIn, where they might seek potential investors.

As with any research method, students should consider the ethics of using social media for research. The most important aspect of social media research is whether the content is public and searchable on the web or semiprivate such as with Facebook Groups that require an administrator's permission to join the group (Beninger, 2016).

Primary Research Example: Shared Photo Album

While the two previous examples took advantage of existing primary research, this example encourages students to collect samples via photos and store them in a shared class album. As open pedagogy principles preach, creating a collective data source for and by students empowers them to own their learning process. Photosharing research hits the "ubiquitous" characteristic of fluid learning, which accounts for learning that can occur at any time and in any situation (Fang, 2014). In a graduate-level agricultural sciences course, students kept a running Google Doc of photos showing different stages of plant development with text annotations, which the professor checked for accuracy and then included in the lecture (Jahnke & Liebscher, 2020). While this individual photo-based primary research was brought into the collective class space, consider how students could also do similar individual analysis from a shared photo album. This shared archive also allows good practice in adding photo credits and descriptions to photos that students are then responsible for citing.

If you decide to have a shared photo album as a source of data collection, it may work best to set up the shared album space and briefly guide students through how to share photos to the album and add descriptions (photographer's name, text description, location, course relevance, tags). You could get quick feedback from students on which photo sharing apps may work best, but ultimately choose one that works well across devices and will likely be familiar to students, such as Google Photos, Google Drive, or Flickr. Have students practice adding a photo early in this process to ensure everyone knows how to do it and can engage in the activity equally, preferably during class time so that you can provide timely feedback and assistance. A scavenger hunt activity can work well in this capacity. Provide a link to the photo album in the LMS or course page and encourage students to make the photo album easy to locate on their phones.

As I encourage with other mobile learning activities, if a couple of students have a significant barrier to engaging in this type of activity, consider roles they can take that focus less on the mobile aspect, such as being the album curator who ensures photos have complete descriptions or considers ways to organize photos into folders or with tags.

References

Alvarez Vazquez, E., Cortes-Mendez, M., Striker, R., Singelmann, L., Pearson, M., & Swartz, E. M. (2020, June). Lessons learned using Slack in engineering education: An innovation-based learning approach. *2020 ASEE Virtual Annual Conference Content Access.* https://doi.org/10.18260/1-2--34916

Barton, M., & Klint, K. (2011). A student's guide to collaborative writing technologies. In Lowe, C., & Zemliansky, P. (Eds.), *Writing spaces: Readings on writing* (Vol. 2; pp. 320–332). Parlor Press.

Beninger, K. (2016). Social media users' views on the ethics of social media research. In A. Quan-Haase & L. Sloan (Eds.), *The SAGE handbook of social media research methods* (pp. 57–73). SAGE. https://doi.org/10.4135/9781473983847

Colin, M., Eastman, S., Merrill, M., & Rockey, A. (2021, March 19). Leveraging mobile technology to achieve teaching goals. *EDUCAUSE Review*. https://er.educause.edu/articles/2021/3/leveraging-mobile-technology-to-achieve-teaching-goals

Dennen, V., & Hao, S. (2014). Intentionally mobile pedagogy: The M-COPE framework for mobile learning in higher education. *Technology, Pedagogy, and Education, 23*(3), 397–419. https://doi.org/10.1080/1475939X.2014.943278

Dodsworth, E., & Nicholson, A. (2012). Academic uses of Google Earth and Google Maps in a library setting. *Information Technology and Libraries (Online), 31*(2), 102–117. https://www.proquest.com/scholarly-journals/academic-uses-google-earth-maps-library-setting/docview/1022030081/se-2

Fang, B. (2014, October 13). Creating a fluid learning environment. *EDUCAUSE Review*. https://er.educause.edu/articles/2014/10/creating-a-fluid-learning-environment

Folk, M. (2016). Kairotic aurality: Audio essays, QR codes, and real audiences. In C. Lutkewitte (Ed.), *Mobile technologies and the writing classroom: Resources for teachers* (pp. 36–51). National Council of Teachers of English.

Jahnke, I., & Liebscher, J. (2020). Three types of integrated course designs for using mobile technologies to support creativity in higher education. *Computers & Education, 146*, 103782. https://doi.org/10.1016/J.COMPEDU.2019.103782

Larry Kushner and Eileen Kushner. (2016, September 16). *StoryCorps*. https://storycorps.org/stories/larry-kushner-and-eileen-kushner-160916/

McIntire-Strasburg, J. (2021, February 15). Forage the urban bounty: 11 crowd-sourced maps of edible plants. *Insteading*. https://insteading.com/blog/forage-the-urban-bounty-11-crowdsourced-maps-of-edible-plants/

Moore, C. (2016). Making a mobile composition kit: Project for testing the waters. In C. Lutkewitte (Ed.), *Mobile technologies and the writing classroom: Resources for teachers* (pp. 5–21). National Council of Teachers of English.

Moore, C. M. (2021). *How faculty use online social spaces to develop their teaching practices: An ethnographic study of the #ungrading online community* [Dissertation, Oakland University]. ProQuest Dissertations Publishing.

Moore, C. (n.d.). Teaching resources: Teaching collections. *Center for Excellence in Teaching and Learning, Oakland University*. https://www.oakland.edu/cetl/teaching-resources/

Pacansky-Brock, M., & Leafstedt, J. (2016, October 6). A step-by-step guide to 'untethered' faculty development. *EdSurge*. https://www.edsurge.com/news/2016-10-06-a-step-by-step-guide-to-untethered-faculty-development

Pew Research Center. (2019, November 20). *Mobile divides in emerging economies*. www.pewresearch.org/internet/2019/11/20/mobile-divides-in-emerging-economies/

Pew Research Center. (2021, April 17). *Mobile facts sheet (2021)*. pewresearch.org/internet/fact-sheet/mobile/

Ralph Catania and Colbert Williams. (n.d.). *StoryCorps*. https://storycorps.org/stories/ralph-catania-and-colbert-williams/

St. Amour, M. (2020, September 16). The moment is primed for asynchronous learning. *Inside Higher Ed*. https://www.insidehighered.com/news/2020/09/16/dont-dismiss-asynchronous-learning-experts-say-improve-it

Udalova, K. (2022, March 3). 4 microlearning examples you can use now to improve training content. *7taps Blog*. https://www.7taps.com/blog/4-microlearning-examples-you-can-use-now-to-improve-training-content

Vie, S. (2016). Critical literacies in mobile social games: Terms of service, privacy policies, and game analysis. In C. Lutkewitte (Ed.), *Mobile technologies and the writing classroom: Resources for teachers* (pp. 82–98). National Council of Teachers of English.

Walwema, J. (2021). The WHO health alert: Communicating a global pandemic with WhatsApp. *Journal of Business and Technical Communication, 35*(1), 35–40. https://doi.org/10.1177/1050651920958507

Washington, A. (2022, March 29). Oakland Mall's new owner takes to TikTok to fill vacant storefronts. *Detroit Metro Times*. https://www.metrotimes.com/news/oakland-malls-new-owner-takes-to-tiktok-to-fill-vacant-storefronts-29666835

CONCLUSION

N ear the end of writing this book, I read *Four Thousand Weeks: Time Management for Mortals* (Burkeman, 2021) as an e-book library loan. I have been getting better at organizing my mobile book notes, but I found myself selecting excerpts and sharing them to my private Slack channel, my "mobile junk drawer." I took notes with some excerpts and not with others. In the book Burkeman reflected on living our short lives in a thoughtful, feasible balance of meaning and finiteness. He discussed distraction, particularly how distraction can disguise itself as productivity when channeled toward the things that don't truly matter. He always came back to deep intention, whether talking about our approach to work or to leisure: "The crucial point isn't that it's wrong to choose to spend your time relaxing, whether at the beach or on BuzzFeed. It's that the distracted person isn't really choosing at all" (n.p.). We have generally come to accept that phones are distraction, that we go to the devices without intention beyond a quick answer. The more we learn about the attention economy and surveillance capitalism, the more we start to feel like there is no choice in the matter of phone distraction. Instead, we can help ourselves and students understand our mobile learning choices, whether it is to be "the distracted person [who] isn't really choosing at all" or the person who has rewired our habits to learn intentionally on phones. In doing so, we may start pushing back on the more deleterious aspects of our phones.

I always come back to being mobile-*mindful*. "Mindful" is paying attention to mobile learning opportunities and barriers. It is intentionally designing such opportunities to get the most out of frequent, bite-sized, ubiquitous, multimodal learning afforded by smartphones. A mobile-mindful mindset even means we recognize the need to move toward and away from screens in the learning process while keeping each part connected. Mobile-mindfulness challenges us to learn on the move, to recognize and capture how the things we are learning in formal institutions live in the places and people around us.

This book is meant to be a balance of providing structure to start adding mobile-mindful options and inviting you to explore your own way into mobile learning. I humbly offer this book as a conversation starter. For all of the words written here, I find myself still intimidated at the prospect of designing whole courses for mobile learning. Nevertheless, I also believe in the power of taking a few steps at a time, seeing how things go, sharing mobile-mindful options with students, and seeing the ideas and practices grow. We are ready to explore the possibilities slowly and sustainably. We will find what has always been true of technology and teaching: If good teachers and thoughtful educators approach tech with a pedagogy-first mindset, they will find exciting possibilities in learning wherever they go. Countless teachers have approached online teaching with some trepidation only to become obsessed with how flexible and creative online learning can be. The same can happen when approaching mobile learning with curiosity. In writing this book, I believe others will be nudged to share the incredible mobile learning work they have done, which is why I look forward to continuing the mobile-mindful learning conversation at the website companion for this book (christinamoorephd.com/MobileMindful).

Reference

Burkeman, O. (2021). *Four thousand weeks: Time management for mortals*. Farrar, Straus, and Giroux.

Fluid Learning Analysis of Your Course

This is an example of how one might fill out the Fluid Learning Analysis activity.

Readings (textbooks, articles)

1. *For the Common Good: A New History of Higher Education in America,* book by Charles Dorn
   - ☑ **Computer** (laptop, desktop)
   - ☑ **Print**
   - ☑ **Mobile** (smartphone, tablet)

   Other Notes (How could this activity increase fluid learning opportunities while maintaining the learning purpose and outcomes?): *I currently only have this listed on my syllabus as a print book ($26 on Amazon), but a student asked permission to buy the Kindle version, which was $6. I told her she could, but I admit I was concerned at how well students would be able to refer to portions of the text during class discussion. In the end, the type of reading we're doing may not require such close reading analysis, and students will be required to read only about half of the book. Therefore, I think I should note that there is a Kindle option, perhaps with a recommendation to use annotation tools that will be useful to writing assignments.*

Multimodal instructional material (video, podcast, exhibit)

2. What Inclusive Teachers Do episode of Teaching in Higher Ed podcast
   - ☑ **Computer** (laptop, desktop)
   - ☑ **Print**
   - ☑ **Mobile** (smartphone, tablet)

Other Notes (How could this activity increase fluid learning opportunities while maintaining the learning purpose and outcomes?): *While clearly an audio format, this podcast episode has a transcript that could be downloaded and printed for reading. The Resources section of the episode also lists a blog post with this same topic and the guest as an author, so based on the purpose of assigning this podcast, I think I should offer the option for people to read the transcript or read two of the listed resources.*

Class activities (worksheets, labs, group activities)

3. *Challenge activities*
   ☑ **Computer** (laptop, desktop)
   ☐ **Print**
   ☐ **Mobile** (smartphone, tablet)
   Other Notes (How could this activity increase fluid learning opportunities while maintaining the learning purpose and outcomes?): *Typically, students progress through a list of "challenges"—or specific tasks students must do to demonstrate their grasp of a skill—that practice applying concepts from instructional videos. After students complete a challenge, I review it before they proceed to the next one. By doing challenges in Google Docs on a laptop in small groups, I can see how students are doing and intervene if support is needed. Therefore, this really works best on laptops, and the assignment is set up to only need one laptop per group (and I ask students what tech they typically have with them at the beginning of each semester). That being said, I think I should always have some print copies with QR codes available so that students can follow along as needed.*

Assessments (quizzes, discussions, exhibit)

4. *End-of-week review quizzes*
   ☑ **Computer** (laptop, desktop)
   ☐ **Print**
   ☑ **Mobile** (smartphone, tablet)
   Other Notes (How could this activity increase fluid learning opportunities while maintaining the learning purpose and outcomes?): *This 10- to 20-question weekly quiz prompts students to check their understanding of class concepts reviewed that week and connects concepts to previous weeks. I also include one or two final open response questions that are feedback*

for me. I always have students do it after class with the idea that this better measures what students remember at least a few hours after class, but now I'm wondering how sound that practice is. Are there some merits to instead allowing the last 10 minutes of class to have students do it on whatever device they want, or will they just rush through it? Also, now that I've tested this on my phone, the quiz questions occasionally come out wonky if I do it through a browser rather than the LMS app, so I may remind students that if they are on a phone they should use the app.

Recommended Apps

Apps listed here are either free or "freemium" (free with an option to pay for a premium version). Search for the name of each app in your phone's app marketplace (e.g., Apple App store, Google Play) and browse its description and ratings. The following list is not comprehensive but shows apps referred to throughout the book plus others, organized into mobile-mindful categories. These choices lean toward those that are generally accessible according to cost, familiarity, integration, and usability across devices. For educational technology that receives higher marks on ethical issues related to how user data is used, see recommendations such as those offered in the Ethical EdTech Wiki (https://ethicaledtech.info/) or consult resources from groups who lead this work (Caines & Glass, 2019).

Curation

- Instapaper
- Diigo
- Google Drive
- Pocket
- Microsoft One Drive
- Pinterest

Documentation and Note-Taking

- Google Keep
- Google Docs
- Google Lens
- Apple Notes
- Microsoft One Note
- Evernote

- Simple Note
- Notability

Multimedia Platforms

- Video: YouTube, Vimeo
- Audio: Podcasts are available on many apps, from those specific to podcasts (PodBean, Google Podcasts, Apple Podcasts) to those that include a broader range of audio (Spotify, SoundCloud)
- Photo: Flickr, Google Photos
- Canva offers mobile-first presentations, including talking presentations as a form of narrated slides
- Google Maps allows users to create interactive maps

Social Learning and Community Building

- Discord
- GroupMe
- Slack
- Microsoft Teams
- Social Media: Facebook, Twitter, Instagram, LinkedIn, Twitter, Tiktok, Pinterest
- Mighty Networks

Mobile Learning Tools

- Alpe Audio and Listenable to develop audio courses
- 7taps for mobile-first microlearning
- QR code generators

Recall and Quizzing

- Google Forms
- Quizlet
- Anki
- Kahoot
- Poll Everywhere
- Mentimeter

Task and Time Management

- Remind is a commonly used app teachers use to send out text reminders to students. The following apps are for managing your own tasks and projects.
- Todoist
- Google Tasks and Reminders
- Toggl, for tracking time

Collaboration, Teamwork, and Project Management

- Trello
- Asana

ABOUT THE AUTHOR

Christina Moore, PhD, is the associate director of the Center for Excellence in Teaching and Learning at Oakland University and lecturer of writing and rhetoric. She writes about higher education teaching and learning, specifically universal design for learning and learning together online. She enjoys feeding people and taking excursions into sci-fi.

access, considerations of, 2, 4, 12–19, 39, 73–76, 79, 83–84, 128
accessibility
    captions and transcripts, 44, 88, 106, 107, 133
    digital accessibility, 3, 12, 75–76, 87–88, 131–133
    digital accessibility checklist, 131–133
    text description, 47, 88, 106, 132, 155
    time, in relation to, 15–16, 38, 76, 95
    web content accessibility guidelines (WCAG), 87–88, 117
active reading, 26, 38, 40, 105
Allen, David, 54
Alvarez Vazquez, Enrique, 98, 151
American Indian College Fund, 28
annotation, 35, 36, 105–106, 116
asynchronous learning, 81, 102, 118–119
Atske, Sara, 13
attention, 7, 14, 19, 59, 79–80, 85–86, 159. *See also* distraction
audience response systems, 7, 80
audiobooks, 38, 67, 116
audio learning
    audio courses, 41–42, 67, 153
    audio reading, 40, 106, 116
    discussion of, 38–42, 44, 67, 104, 106–107, 147
    narrated slides, 38–39, 75, 106, 118, 120
augmented reality, 4, 37, 148

Barre, Betsy, 89, 95
Barron, Brigid, 11, 61

Barton, Matt, 144
Behling, Kirsten, 10, 23
Beninger, Kelsey, 154
Benjamin, Ruha, 84
Bloom's taxonomy, 57, 78
Bowen, José, 79, 86, 87
boyd, danah 7, 102
brain processes in learning
    chunking, 16, 41
    diffuse mode, 16, 18, 53
    discussion of, 16, 40
    distributed practice, 16, 58, 77
    focused learning, 16, 18
    spaced repetition, 16, 57–58, 101
Burkeman, Oliver, 159

Caines, Autumm, 85, 165
Cassata, Cathy 28
CAST, 10
Catania, Ralph, 153
Cavanagh, Sarah Rose, 46
Center for Humane Technology, 26, 60, 109
Centre for Community Organizations, 97
Cohn, Jenae, 34, 92, 100, 117, 124, 134
collaboration
    in classwork and discussion, 118, 144–145
    with academic technologists and instructional designers, 4, 88, 107, 110, 127
Colin, Mindy, 85, 151
communication tools, 46–47, 86–87, 98–99, 110, 119, 126–128, 146
Costa, Karen, 107

COVID-19 pandemic, 1, 28, 35, 47, 74, 148
critical thinking, 7–8, 16, 57
curation, 1, 24, 31, 43, 48, 51–57, 61–64, 67, 77, 134–135, 140

Darby, Flower, 23
Dennen, Vanessa, 83, 86, 139, 151
Deschaine, Mark, 51, 53
digital habits, 24, 26, 28–29, 68, 109, 159
digital reading, 33–36, 104–106, 125. *See also* e-books
Discord, 46–48, 60, 86–87, 97–98, 119, 126–127, 146, 166
distraction, 7, 14–15, 26, 68, 79–80, 159. *See also* attention
diversity and inclusion, 2, 13–14, 16, 79, 125, 131–132
Dodsworth, Eva, 150
Doyle, Terry, 39
Duhigg, Charles, 17

e-books, 35–36, 116, 159
EDUCAUSE Center for Analysis and Research, 1, 14
ethical considerations, 3, 17, 73, 82–85, 99, 108, 110, 139, 152
executive functions, 59, 68, 87, 108–109
experiential learning, 10, 81, 130–131, 141, 152

Fang, Berlin, 9, 11, 12, 61, 122, 123, 155
flashcard apps, 8, 16, 57–59, 68, 107, 108, 123, 126
fluid learning
  applications to mobile learning, 4, 8, 9–11, 12, 26, 27, 34, 35–36, 38, 42, 52, 61–66, 80, 83, 93, 118, 123–124, 134, 161
  discussion of principles, 11, 45, 61, 122
  granularity, 4, 8, 11, 12, 35, 66, 73, 105, 123

interactivity, 11, 45, 62, 65, 71, 107, 117, 122, 123, 137, 145, 149, 151
  neutrality, 11, 52, 61, 66, 76–77, 106, 123
  portability, 9, 11, 61, 66, 123, 142
  ubiquity, 9, 11, 17, 45, 62, 98, 123, 152, 155
Folk, Moe, 147
Franchini, Billie, 130

Gachago, Daniela, 39
Galanek, Joseph, 14, 79, 125
Getting Things Done (GTD), 54
Gierdowski, Dana, 7, 13, 93
Gilliard, Chris, 83, 84
Glass, Erin, 85, 165
Goldstein, Jamie, 28
Google
  Calendar, 61, 94
  Docs, 43, 56, 61, 77, 140, 155, 165
  Drive, 32, 77, 126, 142, 165
  Forms, 78, 82, 152, 166
  Keep, 52, 54, 135, 165
  Lens, 37, 47, 165
  Maps, 117, 150–151, 166
  Reminders, 61, 94, 167
  Tasks, 53, 60, 61, 94, 126, 167

Hao, Shuang, 6, 83, 86, 139, 151
Hart, Carol, 38–39, 116–117
Hokanson, Brad, 23, 51
Hollett, Ty, 11
Honeycutt, Barbi, 39, 41
Hrach, Susan, 9, 18

indigenous communities, 28
inequities, 14, 83
Instapaper, 32–33 52–54, 64–66, 165
intention, 4, 7, 24, 26–27, 41, 43, 68, 87, 137, 159

Jahnke, Isa, 155
Jemisin, N.K., 37
Johnson, Jay, 28

Kalir, Jeremiah 11
Klint, Karl, 144
Kindle, 35–36, 116, 161
Kolb, David, 81, 130
Kushner, Larry and Eileen, 153

Lalonde, Clint, 48
Lang, James, 7, 14, 79
Leafstedt, Jill, 149
learning ecologies
    applications to mobile learning, 23,
        45, 61–66, 99
    discussion of principles, 10–11, 61,
        139–140
    formal learning, 11, 45, 66, 81, 92,
        159
    nonformal learning, 11, 45, 62
    informal learning, 11, 61, 66, 97
learning in motion, 9–10, 18
learning management system (LMS),
        3, 12, 73–77, 87, 88, 93, 95, 98,
        105, 108, 116, 127, 134–135
Levintin, Daniel, 17, 59
Levy, Jenna, 13
Liebscher, Julia, 155
Los Angeles Pacific University, 4

maps, 42, 71, 117, 150–151, 166
Mårtensson, Katarina, 48
Marwick, Alice, 102
McCormick, Alexander, 15
McIntire-Strasburg, Jeff, 151
microlearning, 4, 12, 106, 118, 166
Microsoft Office, 76, 117–118
Microsoft Teams, 48, 86, 97–98,
        126–127, 166
Mighty Networks, 46, 48, 166
Miller, Michelle, 1–2, 16, 34, 43, 57, 92
mobile learning
    definition of, 9–11, 17, 23
    distinction of mobile-mindful
        approach, 9–12, 17, 19, 26, 68,
        87, 109–110, 159
    mobile-first design, 4, 10, 12,
        104–110, 147–148, 166

Mobile Learning Kit, 137–139
    skepticism of, 1, 4, 7–9, 14–15, 26,
        33–34
    student feedback about, 14, 92–94,
        128, 141
modalities, 24, 36, 44, 74, 106–107,
        117, 123, 125, 147
Moore, Shaun, 118–119
Morris, Sean Michael, 145
Mueller, Pam, 34
Murray, Orin, 45

Nave, Lillian, 39
Nichols, Randy, 53
Nicholson, Andrew 150
note-taking, 1, 32, 34–38, 43–44,
        52–56, 67, 94, 105, 116, 135,
        159, 165
notifications, 26–27, 32, 59–61,
        68, 75, 85–87, 99, 108, 110,
        127–128, 134, 146

Oakley, Barbara, 16
offline learning, 10, 36, 84, 95, 109,
        120, 130, 141
Olcese, Nicole, 45
O'Neil, Cathy, 84
online learning, 2, 23, 118, 160
Online Learning Consortium, 107
Oppenheimer, Daniel, 34

Pacansky-Brock, Michelle, 149
Pang, Alex Soojung-Kim, 28
Paul, Annie Murphy, 9, 18, 28, 36
Perrin, Andrew, 13, 83
Pew Research Center, 12, 13, 83,
        92, 148
photos, 25, 37, 42–43, 44, 47, 54, 58,
        67, 102, 106, 126, 138,141–142,
        149, 155, 166
place-based learning, 7, 10, 18, 27–28,
        123
podcasts, 26, 29, 38–41, 44, 67, 95,
        107, 161, 166
polls, 79, 82, 101, 166

Poly-Droulard, Lynda, 38–39, 120
print, 3, 26, 34–38, 40, 47, 59, 80, 84,
    109, 116, 125, 161
privacy, 84–85, 100, 103, 117, 126,
    129, 134, 151–152

QR codes, 24–25, 37, 56, 80, 82, 89,
    105, 109, 122, 124, 130, 131,
    137, 139, 144, 147, 152, 166

Read, Dianna Lai, 4
research methods, 85, 151–152
retrieval practice, 8, 16, 57–59, 67, 76,
    77–78, 104, 107–108, 120–121
Richmond, Nancy, 48
Riha, Helena, 127
Robson, James, 48
Robson, Linda, 16, 17
Rockey, Alex, 59, 108
Rogers, Kristen, 28
Roxå, Torgny, 48
Rutledge, Amy, 108

Seilhamer, Ryan, 6, 9, 13–14, 83, 86
Sejnowski, Terrence, 16
Selfe, Cynthia, 8, 23, 83, 92
Sharma, Sue Ann, 51, 53
Sidhu, Preety, 13
Slack, 46–48, 55, 60, 97, 98, 119, 127,
    146, 151, 166
smartphones
    demographics of ownership, 12-14
    dependency upon to access the
        internet, 12–13, 148
    See also mobile learning
smartwatch, 27
Smydra, Rachel, 39
social learning, 26, 45–47, 67, 97–103,
    166
social media
    applications to mobile learning,
        11, 45–49, 56, 61–64, 67, 97,
        99-103, 110, 117, 119, 133–134,
        145–146, 151, 154, 166

ethical and privacy considerations,
    84–85, 100, 117, 126, 134,
    151–152
Facebook, 26, 45, 47, 48, 97, 100,
    152, 154, 166
Instagram, 47, 117, 154, 166
LinkedIn, 45, 46, 119, 145, 166
Pinterest, 52, 53, 78, 165, 166
Snapchat, 58, 108, 166
TikTok, 45, 48, 100, 154, 166
Twitter, 43, 45–46, 52, 53, 62–64,
    97, 100, 103, 142, 145–146,
    154, 166
Stachowiak, Bonni, 23, 86, 87, 89
Stein, Joel, 45
StoryCorps, 153
student response systems, 7, 80–82
Su, Chiaoning, 148
Supiano, Beckie, 4
syllabus
    mobile-mindful considerations, 73,
        76, 84, 85, 93, 115, 123–126,
        131, 143–144
    technology policy, 79, 125

Tamir, Diana, 43, 54
Thomasson, Kelly, 58
Thompson, VaNessa, 103
Tobin, Thomas, 10, 23
transparency in teaching and learning
    (TILT), 95

Udalova, Kate, 12, 148
universal design for learning (UDL)
    action and expression, 10, 19, 44,
        99, 100, 117
    applications to mobile learning, 38,
        89, 99
    discussion of principles, 10–11,
        17, 19
    engagement, 10, 76, 89, 142–143,
        147
    representation, 10. *See also*
        modalities

University of Central Florida (UCF), 6,
    13–14, 83, 86, 129–130, 138

video, 18, 31, 42–45, 48, 67, 77, 84,
    95, 101–102, 104, 106–107, 119,
    121, 126, 133, 161, 166
Vie, Stephanie, 85, 151–152
visual learning, 42–44, 47, 52, 67, 101,
    106–107, 150
Vogels, Emily, 84
voice-to-text, 1, 32, 36–37, 43, 55, 75,
    98

Wake Forest University, 89, 95
Walker, Mason, 76

Walwema, Josephine, 53, 148
Washington, Alex, 154
web extensions, 32–33, 52
Wesch, Michael, 39
WhatsApp, 148
Williams, Colbert, 153
Wilmer, Henry, 14
Winkelmes, Mary-Ann, 95
workload, 89, 95, 110

YouTube, 31, 42, 43–44, 53, 76–77,
    119, 121, 126, 166

Zlotogorski, Yehoshua, 41, 107

EVIDENCE-BASED
PRINCIPLES AND STRATEGIES

Simone C. O. Conceição
and Les L. Howles

FOREWORD BY B. JEAN MANDERNACH

Designing the Online Learning Experience

Evidence-Based Principles and Strategies

Simone C. O. Conceição and Les L. Howles

Foreword by B. Jean Mandernach

"COVID-19 has pushed education at all levels over the tipping point for online education. This book provides an innovative framework and strategies that bring together user experience, human factors, and design thinking to create a model that wraps around the online learner. Conceição and Howles draw on their experiences as both scholars and practitioners to create a holistic way to think about learning. Both newcomers and experienced online instructors and designers will find creative solutions and strategies to make online teaching more engaging, personalized, and meaningful. The authors share, in this book, a map to the future of online teaching and learning."—*Michelle Glowacki-Dudka, Professor of Adult, Higher, and Community Education Educational Studies; Ball State University*

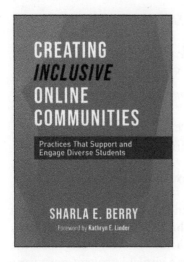

Creating *Inclusive* Online Communities

Practices That Support and Engage Diverse Students

Sharla E. Berry

Foreword by Kathryn E. Linder

Before the COVID-19 pandemic, online and distance education enrolled over 19 million students in the United States. As colleges and universities return to in-person instruction, the number of online courses and programs is poised to grow exponentially. At the same time, institutions of higher education are increasingly more diverse—racially, ethnically, and socioeconomically—with present and future students having a range of intersectional needs related to their cultural backgrounds, gendered experiences, and abilities. Sharla Berry offers faculty practical strategies for building asynchronous, synchronous, and blended online courses and programs that are inclusive and engaging for diverse learners.

Recognizing that community is a complex, contextual, and constantly shifting concept, Sharla Berry opens this book by addressing how to develop an inclusive approach to online teaching that takes into account the experiences and needs of historically marginalized and underrepresented students. Covering the affordances and limitations of synchronous and asynchronous teaching, as well as hybrid and fully online instruction, she outlines different approaches to course design, and identifies how to use the myriad functions of learning management systems—from collaborative tools to administering tests—to engage students and assess their involvement and progress.

Engaging Virtual Environments

Creative Ideas and Online Tools to Promote Student Interaction, Participation, and Active Learning

Joanne Ricevuto and Laura McLaughlin

Foreword by Lillian Nave

"Ricevuto and McLaughlin provide the rationale behind what it means to be a virtual instructor in every facet that the role entails. They describe the many hats that a virtual instructor must wear in order to design, build, facilitate, and evaluate a collaborative, engaging virtual experience. Each chapter is divided into two sections. The first part of each chapter explores the related roles or facets of a virtual instructor, and the second section provides tips, tools, and templates to help the instructor in each one of these roles.

This book is a veritable decision tree for the new or 'not-so-new' virtual instructor that includes helpful definitions, appropriate questions to ask oneself along the way, and all of the tips, tools, and templates you could ask for to make teaching online fun and satisfying for the instructor, and interesting and engaging for the student. It is an essential tool to have in the virtual instructor's toolbox for today's challenging online teaching and learning environment."—*From the Foreword by* **Lillian Nave**

Continued from following page

your smartphone, and without a major investment of time, demonstrating the simple steps she took to develop her bank of videos and build her confidence to deliver short, straightforward learning aids that are effective and personal. Embedded QR codes in the text enable you to view sample videos and screencasts that bring the book's advice to life as you read.

If you've been wanting to include videos in your teaching but haven't found the time or confidence, this book will help you to develop a simple and sustainable video development process, supporting both your success and the success of your students.

Also available from Stylus

99 Tips for Creating Simple and Sustainable Educational Videos

A Guide for Online Teachers and Flipped Classes

Karen Costa

Foreword by Michelle Pacansky-Brock

"Reading *99 Tips for Creating Simple and Sustainable Educational Videos* is like sitting down with an old friend and learning all of her best strategies for producing video content that will both help and motivate students in their learning. I loved the simplicity and practicality of Costa's suggestions and think that this is the perfect book for instructors who want to dip their toes in the video production waters, but are not sure where to start."—*Kathryn E. Linder*, *Executive Director of Program Development, Kansas State University Global Campus*

The research is clear: Online learning works best when faculty build regular, positive, and interactive relationships with students. A strategy that helps forge such a relationship is the use of videos. Student satisfaction and course engagement levels also increase with the use of instructor-generated videos—the subject of this book.

Beginning by outlining the different types of videos you can create, and what the research says about their effectiveness, Karen Costa explains how they can be designed to reinforce learning, to align with and promote course outcomes, and to save you time across your courses. She then describes how to create successful videos with commonly available technologies such as

Continues on previous page

22883 Quicksilver Drive
Sterling, VA 20166-2019

Subscribe to our email alerts: www.Styluspub.com